*Language in South Asian Society*

# ENGLISH IN INDIAN BILINGUALISM

LANGUAGE IN SOUTH ASIAN SOCIETY

*Series Editors:* BRAJ B. KACHRU and S.N. SRIDHAR

---

# ENGLISH IN INDIAN BILINGUALISM

KAMAL K. SRIDHAR
State University of New York
at Stony Brook

MANOHAR
2026

First published 1989
Reprinted 2026
First eBook edition 2026



ISBN 978-81-85054-67-4 (hardbound)
ISBN 978-93-7451-367-5 (eBook)

*Published by*
Ajay Kumar Jain *for*
Manohar Publishers & Distributors
4753/23 Ansari Road, Daryaganj
New Delhi 110 002

Printed and bound in India

**For**

*Braj and Yamuna Kachru*

**pite:va putrasya sakhe:va sakhyuhu**

# Foreword

A native of India goes abroad in search of new horizons and trained at an American University in linguistics and language education, cannot ignore the call of the "old country": it draws the adventurer back into its spell, an incomparable laboratory for never-ending stimulus and research. Kamal Sridhar studied in a very American milieu, the Midwestern University of Illinois at Urbana-Champaign, and after her studies has been teaching in New York, first at Queens College and now at the State University of New York at Stony Brook. She is married to a fine scholar, S.N. Sridhar, likewise from India, a native speaker of Kannada, a former student of the well-known psycholinguist Charles Osgood, and the two Sridhars, whether individually or as a team, work always, and with success, on the language problems of India.

Kamal Sridhar is bringing together, in the volume at hand, ten of her studies dealing, essentially, with the role of English in India. She approaches a multifaceted topic from varying angles and writes with empathy and firsthand knowledge, and what makes this collection particularly interesting is the far-reaching validity of her observations, a typology of bilingualism, this dynamic subfield of sociolinguistics, which evolves from her India-centered case histories.

Indian English, although acquired through formal instruction, is, as Sridhar emphasizes time and again, a living variety of English, and as a living, "nativized" language it is beyond the stage of being subjected to an ongoing assessment as to being good or bad, correct or incorrect English. In this respect, as in many others, the English of India reminds us of that other superlanguage, Latin of the Middle Ages: there was no right or wrong pronunciation of it, and its grammar often reflected a speaker's native grammar. But when the

## Foreword

Humanists of the Renaissance insisted on "correctness", Latin turned from a living into a dead language.

India, as a multilingual society, assigns to its languages specific roles: a speaker's regional language, the "mother tongue", functions as the language of the intimate domain. Two superregional languages constitute the diglossic pattern of H and L, high and low, and in this sociolinguistic structure English represnts H and Hindi, L English is in India, as in all cultures where it functions as the "second language", the language of Westernization and modernism, i.e., of middle-class life, business, technology, industry, and democracy. It is the key to success. Codemixing with English (the insertion of English into non-English speech) suggests up-to-dateness and prestige.

This vital function of English, as described by Sridhar, reminds us of the English incessantly imposed on the immigrant in the United States who belongs to a linguistic minority: while the minority language remains the language of the "intimate domain", for a long time doomed to surface in pronunciation, phrasing, and codemixing, English is the link to middle-calss life. In two of her essays, Sridhar touches on this analogy: she investigated, through fieldwork, a group of Kannada-speaking Indians in New York, representing a first-generation of "new ethnics", who were immigrants with superior professional skills. They attributed their success to their proficiency in English.

And in her last and captivating chapter, relying on the deft observations by a well-known Indian writer, Naipaul, she describes the adaptation of Hindi-speaking Indians to their English environment on the West-Indian island of Trinidad. The new-comers are still in an early stage of their second-language acquisition, yet their goal is evident: fluency in English as the token of assimilation and upward mobility. A man speaks English to gain the respect of his new, Hindi-speaking relatives: "he always spoke English with his in-laws". And he justifies his shift of language by saying to his wife: "we shouldn't be shame to talk the people language good".

How often, in the course of the last two or three millenia, has this sentence, mutatis mutandis, been uttered by the proud speakers of a prestige language!

Henry Kahane

Department of Linguistics
University of Illinois
Urbana, IL. 61801, U.S.A.
August 20, 1988.

# Contents

# Preface

The chapters in this volume represent a slightly revised and edited version of a selection of my research papers on bilingualism with special reference to Indian bilingualism in English, over the last few years. They explore the theoretical, methodological, empirical, and pedagogical dimensions of bilingualism.

As is well-known, India is one of the classic fields in the world for the study of bilingualism. The presence, sustained over millennia, of hundreds of languages belonging to four different language families, the vast difference in their literary and other types of "development," the checquered socio-cultural history of the area which has witnessed the use of a series of Pan-Indian elite link languages, the long tradition of assimilation, adaptation and convergence of languages and cultures, the challenges of the current gigantic experiment in building a multilingual, pluralistic nation committed to democracy--these are but a few of the characteristics of Indian society and culture that make it a fascinating area for the study of bilingualism.

Against this background, English plays a vital role in the Indian communication network, both in the context of individual and societal bilingualism. It is crucial in such areas as higher education in science and technology, in higher level administration, the legal system, in inter-regional communication, in the mass media, and in the revitalization of Indian languages and literatures. It is a coveted asset on an individual level, the ticket to upward mobility, but also a convenient target of political posturing. It is a buffer against Hindi for South Indians, and an impediment to nationalistic assertion for some protagonists of Hindi. It is an essential ingredient of the contemporary educated Indian's conversational style. It has been a major influence on, and has been deeply influenced by Indian languages. It is a major player in the language ecology of contemporary India.

It is this intersection of Indian bilingualism and English that forms the domain of this volume. Needless to say, the studies presented here examine only the tip of the proverbial iceberg. Nevertheless, they deal with a wide range of topics and issues, such as the distinctive characteristics of Indian bilingualism, the range of languages and varieties in which Indians are bilingual, the determinants of language choice in various contexts, the evaluation of the prestige, utility, and emotional associations of the different languages, the interplay of languages in the bilingual's repertoire resulting in code switching and code mixing and the syntactic, sociolinguistic, and psycholinguistic implications of such language interaction, the implications of bilingualism for language policy and its implementation in such areas as education, among others. They also analyse the acquisition and use of Indian English with reference to questions such as the role of mother tongue transfer in second language acquisition, the role of Indian cultural conventions in the performance of speech acts, the typological similarities and differences between indigenized and foreign language varieties of English, the choice of an instructional model for teaching English in India, the syntactic constraints and processing characteristics of English-mixed Indian language varieties, and the literary potential of bilingualism, as well as other related topics.

Although they were written for different occasions, journals and books, there is, I believe, a common thread that runs through them and justifies their coming together in book form. This common thread is a perspective which views the forms and functions of English in India as an organic part of Indian bilingualism. English in India is not just an "additional" language. It exists in a complementing, overlapping, mutually sustaining, inter-penetrating relationship--in short, a symbiotic relationship--with the languages and codes of the Indian bilingual. In developing this organic theory of bilingualism, I have drawn on the insights of a number of disciplines, including sociolinguistics, sociology of language, educational psychology, language policy and planning, psycholinguistics, second language acquisition, pragmatics, and stylistics. I have also tried to demonstrate the need for and the utility of the theory by providing empirical evidence from surveys of language use and attitudes as well as analysis of the formal properties of Indian English. It is my modest hope that this kind of theoretically informed empirical work will contribute to a more insightful understanding of bilingualism in general and of Indian bilingualism and Indian English in particular.

I am very grateful to Professor Henry Kahane, former President of the Linguistic Society of America and an authority on language and cultural contact, for guiding my research over the years and for contributing his kind Foreword. I also wish to thank the American Institute of Indian Studies for their generous subvention for this book, and especially, Dr. Pradeep Mehendiratta, Director, for his friendship and support. I shall not try to say formal thanks to S. N. Sridhar, my husband, colleague, and co-author of Chapters 4 and 6, whose advice, editorial and otherwise, has been most valuable. Thanks also to Frank Anshen, Mark Aronoff, Christina Bethin, Juan Cobarrubias, David Cohen, Joshua Fishman, Fran Kelley, Bh. Krishnamurti, Peter Lowenberg, Larry Smith, Richard Smock, Mima Spencer, and Betty Weidman for their continuing encouragement, counsel, and friendship. Ms. Barbara Kubodera went over the manuscript and Ms. Wanda Olivera prepared the final version--to both of them my appreciation and thanks. Loving thanks to my family, Sona, Saras, Neil, Pappu, and Chinni for all their affection and support; and special hugs to Amita and Shamit for their contribution to my cheer. Above all, I am happy to have this chance to express my fond love and profound gratitude to Braj and Yamuna Kachru for their magnificent support and generosity, intellectual and otherwise, throughout my career.

# List of Tables

# Acknowledgements

Acknowledgements are made to the following publishers from whose texts earlier versions of the chapters have been taken.

Cambridge University Press for "Bilingualism in India: A Profile" in *Annual Review of Applied Linguistics*, 6 (1985). *Canadian Journal of Psychology* for "The Syntax and Psycholinguistics of Bilingual Code Mixing" in 34:4 (1980). The Center for Research on Multilingualism, Brussels, for "Language Policy for Education in Multilingual India: Issues and Implementation" in *Contact + Conflict* (1989). Elsevier/North Holland, Inc., for "Sociolinguistic Theory and Non-Native Varieties of English" in *Lingua* 68 (1985). Georgetown University Press for "Pragmatic Features of Indigenized Varietes: Requesting in Indian English" in Georgetown University Roundtable on Languages and Linguistics 1989. Macmillan, India, for "Cognitive Educational Psychology and Second Language Acquisition Strategies" in *Perspectives on English Language Teaching*, 1986. Mouton, Inc., for "Language Maintenance and Language Shift Among Asian Indians: Kannadigas in the New York Area" in *International Journal of the Sociology of Language* 69 (1988). Pergamon Press, Inc., for "Bridging the Paradigm Gap: Second Language Acquisition Theory and Indigenized Varieties of English" in *World Englishes* 5:1 (1986) and for "English in a South Indian Urban Context" in *The Other Tongue* (1982). The *Journal of Indian Writing* in "English for Bilingualism and the Creative Potential: Language as Medium and Symbol in the Early Novels of V. S. Naipaul" in 15:1 (1987).

# Chapter 1

# Bilingualism in India:
## A Profile

## 1. INTRODUCTION

As a background to the theoretical and empirical studies that follow, I would like to present in this chapter an overview of studies on the Indian bilingual's verbal repertoire and the functional allocation of languages. This is, of course, not easy. The problem lies in the complexity and diversity of the situation, and the danger of inanity resulting from oversimplification. However, since the alternative is to wait for book-length treatments which have yet to be written, I shall compromise by treating only the broadly representative situations and trends and ignoring the (sometimes more interesting) particularities of a given language or an individual contact situation.

### 1.1 Salient Features of Indian Bilingualism

The salient features of bilingualism in India include the following:

(a) the fluidity of language identity, leading to the under-reporting and variable reporting of the extent of bilingualism in the area;

(b) high degree of societal bilingualism, not only in border areas and among the educated population, but on a very widespread scale among the population in general;

(c) high incidence of polyvarietalism and multilingualism, involving regional, social (e.g., caste, occupation, etc.), and institutionalized (e.g., diglossic) varieties on the one hand, and cognate languages as well as unrelated languages, on the other;

(d) the widespread use of 'mixed' language varieties;

(e) the phenomenon of linguistic convergence, i.e., the tendency for languages in contact to adopt one another's formal features, resulting in the formation of the South Asian 'linguistic area'; and

(f) the tendency on the part of minority language speakers to maintain their languages, despite a low level of literacy and inadequate formal language instruction.

For more general discussions of Indian bilingualism, see Emeneau 1974, Weinrich 1957, Pandit 1972, 1977, Southworth and Apte 1974, Kachru and Sridhar 1978, Sharma and Kumar 1977, Kachru 1979, 1982, Gumperz 1958, 1961, Shapiro and Schiffman 1981, Khubchandani 1983, Pattanayak 1981, among others.

## 1.2 Extent of Bilingualism

According to the 1961 census, 15.1% of India's population was bilingual. The corresponding figure for 1971 was 9.7%. (The 1981 census figures are not available.) However, scholars generally agree that both these figures vastly understate the extent of bilingualism in India. The under-reporting is attributed to a variety of factors: speakers are reluctant to claim competence in a language unless they can read and write it; many languages are traditionally regarded simply as dialects of one of the major languages of the region; competence in a non-prestigeful language is not considered worth mentioning; and the 1961 census recorded only two languages other than the mother tongue, while the 1971 census used only the first of the two reported languages to tabulate figures on bilingualism, etc. These and other aspects of the census data have been discussed in Davidson 1969 (for the 1961 census), Kachru (1977), Khubchandani (1983), Dua and Sharma (1977), and others.

The following Table, based on the 1961 census (cf. Khubchandani 1978), illustrates the vast amount of regional variation in the degree of bilingualism in India.

This distribution as well as the presence of substantial numbers of minority language speakers in every state, and in every district, shows that India is a multilingual country not only in a territorial sense (i.e., juxtaposition of monolingual states) but at the "grass-roots level."

**TABLE 1**

*Percentage of Bilingualism in Different States in India (1961)*

| State | Percentage of Population who are Bilinguals |
|---|---|
| Andhra Pradesh | 4.94 |
| Assam | 14.76 |
| Bihar | 5.42 |
| Gujarat | 4.47 |
| Jammu & Kashmir | 6.97 |
| Kerala | 4.94 |
| Madhya Pradesh | 4.21 |
| Madras (Tamil Nadu) | 15.03 |
| Maharashtra | 13.31 |
| Mysore (Karnataka) | 18.84 |
| Orissa | 6.39 |
| Panjab | 9.71 |
| Rajasthan | 3.69 |
| Uttar Pradesh | 3.58 |
| West Bengal | 6.84 |

## 1.3 Bilingualism and Language Variation

Bilingualism in India can not be discussed without taking into account the rather complex pattern of variation within the languages used in the area, especially because such variation is often quantitatively equivalent to inter-language variation elsewhere in the world, and in some cases, the non-mother tongue varieties are formally acquired. The types of variation studied in India include the following: (1) regional varieties (in the case of Hindi, the varieties spoken at the extreme ends of the speech area are mutually unintelligible), (2) caste dialects (cf. Bean 1974, Pattanayak 1975 and the references therein) and religious varieties (Miranda 1978), (3) diglossic variation especially in Dravidian languages (cf. Ferguson 1959, De Silva 1976, Annamalai 1986, Shanmugam Pillai 1965, Gnanasundaram 1983, for Tamil; Nayak 1967, Giraddi 1973, S. N. Sridhar 1980 for Kannada; Krishnamurti 1979a, Radhakrishnan 1980 for Telugu; but also in Bengali, cf. Dimock 1960, Singh and Maniruzzaman 1983, in general, the papers in Krishnamurti 1986; (4) stylistic variation (Persian-based High Urdu and Sanskrit-based High Hindi, as opposed to colloquial Hindi-Urdu; (5) code mixed varieties (cf. Kachru 1979, Southworth 1977 for South Asia in general), (Bhatia 1987, Pandit 1978, Verma 1976, Vaid 1980, Singh 1985 for Hindi), (S. N. Sridhar 1978, Sridhar and Sridhar 1980 for Kannada),

(Annamalai 1971 for Tamil, among others); (6) pidginized contact languages in urban areas (cf. Apte 1974b, Hosali 1982 for Butler English).

## 1.4 The Other Tongues in the Bilingual's Repertoire

Before discussing the languages in the verbal repertoire of the Indian bilingual, it is helpful to define some terms. The term 'official language' is used to refer to the language of the federal government, Hindi. The term 'regional language' refers to the primary language of the linguistically organized states (e.g., Gujarati in Gujarat). In most cases, the regional language is the official language of the state or province in which it is spoken, but not in all cases (e.g., Kashmiri is not the official language of Jammu and Kashmir). The term 'minority language' is used to refer to several rather different entities, including (a) tribal languages, which lack a script or written literature and are not used in education, administration, the media, etc.; (b) the languages of migrants from other linguistic regions, even when these languages are the majority or official languages in their home states, e.g., Tamilians in Maharashtra; (c) the languages spoken by small, non-tribal, non-migrant communities (e.g., Tulu in Karnataka, Konkani in Karnataka, Maharashtra, Goa, and Kerala).

The speaker of a minority language tends to be bilingual in the regional dialect of the dominant language of the area for economic reasons, even if he or she is illiterate. Depending on the extent of schooling attained, he may also know the standard variety of the regional language, as well as Hindi and/or English. Speakers whose mother tongue is a regional language may exhibit one of the following patterns of bilingualism. If the mother tongue is one of the four Dravidian languages of the South, he or she may speak the caste or local dialect, the regional variety, and if educated, he or she may also use the standard variety of the regional language, English, and increasingly, Hindi. For speakers whose mother tongue is one of the many varieties of Hindi, the codes may include, the caste dialect, the regional variety of Hindi, and if educated, Standard Hindi and English. In addition, many Indians speak one or more languages of the minorities in their region, or the language of a neighboring state. Some speakers also learn one of the Classical languages, Sanskrit for Hindus, Arabic (and/or Persian) for Muslims, and Pali for Buddhists. Apart from these individual languages or varieties, many speakers also control mixed varieties such as English-mixed Tamil, Sanskritized Hindi, Persianized Hindi, etc. Thus, the choice of the other tongues in the Indian bilingual's repertoire is determined by (a) the status of his or her mother tongue as a minority, regional or official language; (b) by educational attainment (English is usually introduced in the fifth grade); and (c) his or her membership in social networks as a result of family contacts or the occupational or other roles he or she wishes to play in society.

Of the above types, bilingualism in English, Hindi, and the classical languages are more or less Pan-Indian, while the other types are, of course, regional (Pandit 1977, Khubchandani 1978, 1983, Bhatia 1982, Kachru 1979). As Khubchandani (1978) shows, bilingualism in English is considerably more prevalent than in Hindi [or in the Classical languages], especially in the non- Hindi areas. (See Table 2 below). Bilingualism in English is also a predominantly urban phenomenon. The incidence of bilingualism is substantially higher among the speakers of minority languages (especially tribal languages, cf. Ekka 1979 for Kuruxs, Mahapatra 1979 for Santhali) than among speakers of the regional languages, and least among Hindi speakers. English and the classical languages are learned through formal instruction, while bilingualism in the regional languages and Hindi is acquired as much through informal contact and at school.

**TABLE 2**

*Pan-Indian Bilingualism Pattern:*
*Preferred Second Language of Non-Hindi Speakers*

| State/Territory | Hindi (%) | English (%) |
|---|---|---|
| Andhra Pradesh | 1.7 | 21.2 |
| Assam | 2.4 | 27.4 |
| Bihar | 6.8 | 18.4 |
| Delhi | 29.1 | 52.7 |
| Gujarat | 2.9 | 30.5 |
| Jammu & Kashmir | 8.6 | 11.0 |
| Kerala | 0.2 | 46.8 |
| Madhya Pradesh | 23.1 | 17.1 |
| Maharashtra | 6.6 | 29.8 |
| Mysore | 1.4 | 25.4 |
| Orissa | 0.8 | 21.7 |
| Panjab | 7.4 | 24.2 |
| Tamilnadu | 0.2 | 31.1 |
| Uttar Pradesh | 13.7 | 17.6 |
| West Bengal | 1.2 | 29.3 |

(From Khubchandani 1978:578-79, see also Bhatia 1982:238.)

## 2. FUNCTIONAL ALLOCATION OF CODES

A number of studies of the use of various languages and dialects in different domains have appeared in recent years. Parasher (1980) and Chapter 7 (this volume) are sociolinguistic surveys of the use of English vis-a-vis the regional languages and Hindi in a range of domains in the South Indian cities of Hyderabad and Bangalore, respectively. Ullrich (1982) contrasts the patterns of multilingualism among the Kannada speaking Havyaka brahmins in a Karnataka village and in the state capital, Bangalore. Koul and Schmidt (1983) investigated language use and preference in several formal and informal domains in two areas in Kashmir. Misra and Dua (1980) is a report of the most extensive sociolinguistic survey ever undertaken in South Asia. This survey, conducted by a team of linguists from the Central Institute of Indian Languages, Mysore, studied the patterns of language proficiency, use, and preferences of 2,710 persons from all over the North Indian state of Himachal Pradesh, covering a wide range of domains and population and language samples. It provides an unusually extensive, detailed picture of language use in a multilingual state. Empirical studies of language use in urban areas are also found in the studies of language maintenance and shift conducted by linguists from Delhi University (Pandit 1977, Mukherjee 1980, Satyanath 1982). The following discussion of the functional allocation of codes draws on the findings of all these studies, though it does, of necessity, sacrifice specificity in order to present the overall picture.

I will first discuss the non-formal domains of family, friendship, 'transactions', and religion, and then go on to the formal domains of the mass media, education, law, and administration. In the family domain, the code that is dominant is the speaker's mother tongue in its most intimate variety. This is the caste dialect in most cases, which serves as a symbol of group identity and solidarity. The use of other varieties (or variants) is either actively discouraged (for example, Brahmin children are reprimanded when they substitute the stigmatized unaspirated consonants for aspirated ones) or considered to be pretentious. In the presence of outsiders, however, a more neutral local or regional variety is often employed. In written communication, the regional language is used in the family domain, though English is increasingly used in this domain in educated urban families. Educated urbanites also use a great deal of English in speaking to their friends and colleagues on all kinds of topics, not only those related to work. In rural areas, most transactions (shopping, banking, etc.) are carried out in the regional dialect but correspondence and bookkeeping are in the regional standard. There is a choice between the regional language and English in the urban areas for the educated people in the 'transaction' domain, though some transactions, e.g., banking, elicit more English. In the domain of religion, rituals, recitations, and ceremonies are carried out in the classical language (Sanskrit, Arabic, Pali, etc.), while individual exchanges (e.g., conversations between the priest and the devotees) are conducted in the local variety. Public religious transactions such as mythological narratives, philosophical discourses and speeches are held in the regional (colloquial standard) language, often in a distinct oratorical style. The regional languages and classical languages are used in formal written communications in the domain of religion, though devotional hymns and prayers are often in the regional dialects. In multilingual metropolitan centers like Bombay, Madras, Bangalore, Delhi, etc., public religious discourses are sometimes conducted in English. It is interesting to note parenthetically that several religious periodicals aimed at pan-Indian readership are published in English.

In the mass media, the lion's share is claimed by English, Hindi, and the regional languages, with the regional dialects and minority languages playing a marginal role, if at all, in the oral mode. Although radio news bulletins and special-topic programming is offered in many minority languages and dialects, the major emphasis is on English and Hindi for pan-Indian programs and the regional languages for state-wide programs. This is also true of the print media. The largest number of newspapers and periodicals are in English and Hindi, with the former considered to be the more influential and more widely circulated. Here also the more educated urban dwellers prefer to receive their news and information through English while the moderately educated people rely on the regional language media. In non-Hindi states, the preferred languages for this function are English and the regional languages.

Hindi is extremely popular in the entertainment domain, much more than the regional languages or English. Hindi movies and film songs find wide patronage all over India, and are probably the most effective instruments for the popularization of the language. The regional languages come a distant second, while the role of the minority languages is negligible in this domain. English movies are, again, popular in urban centers.

In the formal domains, a two-tier system is found. The regional dialects, minority languages, and the regional languages are used in spoken communication at the lower levels of administration, courts of law, and education. The regional languages (but not dialects or minority languages) are also used in written communication at the lower levels in these domains, but English is still the preferred choice of language in the written mode and at the higher levels. While regional languages are increasingly being used in education up to the graduate level, English is still the primary medium of instruction at the graduate (or "post-graduate" in Indian English) level, especially in science, engineering, and medicine (see Chapter 2 for a discussion of the current scene in language use in Indian education).

Thus, the minority languages (and regional dialects), regional languages, and English stand in an ascending hierarchy of functional roles, with Hindi in the same position as the regional languages in the Hindi areas and below the regional languages in the non-Hindi areas. The roles of the languages in the repertoire are more complementary in rural areas than in urban centers, and in some domains (e.g., higher education, religion); they are overlapping in others (e.g., friendship, middle level administration, and transactions in the urban areas).

Because of their association with differently valued domains, the use of different languages in the Indian bilingual's repertoire carries different role expectations. English is associated with upward socio-economic mobility, national mobility, authority, modernization, and Westernization. Hindi carries connotations of nationalism and is considered a politically advantageous asset, but it lacks prestige in the non-Hindi areas (see S. N. Sridhar 1987a). (Several of the studies listed earlier show that Hindi would be used with lower-status interlocutors in South India.) The regional languages are symbols of cultural identity and democratic values (English fails on this score). The regional dialects and minority languages are primarily tokens of solidarity at a more local level, but their speakers seem to be quite aware of their limited utility and strive to equip themselves with linguistic skills that would enable them to transcend these limitations. Expanding one's linguistic repertoire as a means to acquiring wider and more valued roles is, of course, seen at all levels.

The overlap in the distribution of functions noted above is interesting because it provides the conditions for the use of mixed codes (see below). It also affects even the traditional complementary distribution of the High and Low varieties in diglossic languages such as Tamil, Kannada, and Telugu. More and more, the functions of the High varieties are being taken over by a modified version of the Low varieties in these languages (see Annamalai 1976, Krishnamurti 1979a, Shanmugam Pillai 1965). At the same time, the register range of the regional languages is being expanded at an explosive rate, and the chief mechanism of this "modernization" process is borrowing, especially from English and Sanskrit (Krishnamurti and Mukherjee 1985). Thus, the educated speakers of Indian languages are called upon to acquire the new highly Sanskritized (except in the case of Tamil, which uses indigenous sources and English for its vocabulary) and Englishized codes for academic and professional uses.

## 3. USE OF MIXED CODES

The studies discussed in the previous section dealt primarily with the use of 'pure' codes--caste dialects, local or regional varieties of languages, and their standard varieties. An important aspect of bilingual language use in South Asia is the use of mixed codes, especially those language types involving the intercalation of elements (words, phrases, sentences) from two separate languages within single sentences. This phenomenon has been referred to variously as 'conversational code switching' (Gumperz 1982), 'code mixing' (Kachru 1979), as well as with language-specific labels such as 'Hinglish' (Verma 1976), and 'Singlish' (Sinhala-English, Fernando 1977) in recent sociolinguistic literature. Code mixing has a long history in Indian literature. The highly Sanskritized style used in traditional Dravidian literatures, e.g., in Malayalam, was referred to as the *manipravala* style. In the Buddhist tradition, it is known as the Buddhist Hybrid Sanskrit (Damsteegt 1978). Code mixing has been recognized as an aspect of the proficient bilinguals' language use, and not necessarily a manifestation of inadequate command of a second language. It has been shown to obey structural constraints on the compatibility of the 'host' and 'guest' elements in the sentence (Annamalai 1978, Sridhar and Sridhar 1980, Desai 1982), and to serve various sociolinguistic and stylistic functions, including addressee specification, interjection, emphasis, reiteration, quotation, message qualification (Gumperz 1982), neutralization of identity (Annamalai 1978), role identification, authentication, or technicalization (Kachru 1978, S. N. Sridhar 1978), among others. These studies also show that the mixing of elements from different languages have different functions--functions which result directly from the association of a given language with specific domains in the community's verbal repertoire. Thus code mixing with English suggests modernization, Westernization, authority, prestige, and knowledgeability; Sanskrit evokes traditional scholarship and classicism; Hindi-Urdu street vernacular in Karnataka symbolizes machismo (S. N. Sridhar 1978). Recent studies have examined this phenomenon in films (Vaid 1980), creative literature (Alam 1983, S. N. Sridhar 1978, Kachru 1983b, Pandharipande 1983), informal conversations (Desai 1982, Shanta 1977, Southworth 1977), and academic discourse (Kumar 1982). Some fascinating implications of code mixing for linguistic theory are explored in Annamalai (1971), and Singh (1985), while Sridhar and Sridhar (1980) discuss its implications for psycholinguistic models of sentence processing. This is one of the most active areas of research in Indian bilingualism at present and rightly so, because India is an excellent testing ground for various types of hypotheses on this topic because of the varieties of bilingual situations found here as well as the coexistence of languages from different families in the South Asian bilingual's verbal repertoire. An important desideratum of research in this area is detailed ethnographic studies of the functions of code mixing in stable urban and rural bilingual communities with different language dyads and populations with different educational and social backgrounds.

## 4. CONCLUSION

In this chapter, I have tried to provide a general account of the types of languages/varieties found in the Indian bilingual's verbal repertoire and the sociolinguistic contexts of their use. There are many other aspects of Indian bilingualism that are relevant to the discussion of this topic--for example, the convergence of languages brought about by code mixing (cf. Gumperz and Wilson 1971, Southworth and Apte 1974, Annamalai (to appear), S. N. Sridhar 1981); the maintenance of the ethnic languages by numerous minorities in restricted domains (cf. Pandit 1972, 1977), especially the myths and reality of such maintenance (cf. Mahapatra 1979, Chapter 9); the controversies in language policy in education, administration, judiciary, etc., the problems in the use of regional languages in formal domains, the recognition and codification of tribal languages, and many others--but each of them is a specialized aspect of language use which requires a separate and detailed study. I do hope that despite the omission of these relevant issues, this chapter will go some way toward giving an overall picture of the complex and fascinating character of bilingualism in India. The best work on Indian bilingualism has yet to be written.

# Chapter 2

# Language Policy for Education in Multilingual India:

## Issues and Implementation

### 1. INTRODUCTION

The study of language policy in education has been essentially atheoretical so far, consisting mainly of case studies of countries or supra- or sub-national regions or ethnic groups. While it is undeniable that each country or ethnic or linguistic community faces highly specific problems and adopts policies resulting from compromises among particular pressure groups, it is also clear that certain constants and recurrences may be identified, if only at an abstract level.

An obvious example of such a constant is the articulation between the legal (official, constitutional) status of the languages and their status in the curriculum as subject or media at the primary, secondary, or university stage, (e.g., English, Hindi, and the regional languages, and the "minority" languages in India). Another constant is the dynamic relationship between educational practice and sociolinguistic reality: for example, a language may have a high status in the educational curriculum but viewed as of little value outside of the school (e.g., Hindi in South India, the foreign languages in the U.S.) or vice versa (e.g., Basque, and numerous Pidgins and Creoles).

There are also recurrent themes and principles that can be easily identified in cross-cultural studies of the subject: the almost universal subscription to the value of the mother-tongue, both on cognitive grounds and emotional; the ancient controversy about the priority of language development versus use in the educational system; the conflict between equity and socio-linguistic pragmatism, which typically arises when speakers of minority (or less powerful) languages have to learn more languages than those of majority (or more powerful) languages, and so on. Many others may be cited. Such cross-cultural similarities support the validity of the attempt to evolve theoretical models of language-for-education policies.

The present chapter has three aims. One is to make an indirect contribution to the theoretical enterprise suggested above by identifying certain substantive issues of theoretical and comparative interest in the evolution of language-in-education policies in India. The second aim is to present a detailed account of the issues in language-for-education policy for India in relation to the Indian socio-political context--especially the themes of colonization, modernization, democracy, and language and ethnic identity. Thirdly, this paper discusses the current scene in the implementation of language-in-education policies with reference to the latest statistics on the use of languages as media of higher education.

The Indian experience in the area of formulating and implementing a language policy for education is interesting for a number of reasons. First, India is a traditionally multilingual society where hundreds of languages belonging to separate language families have coexisted for millennia and this pattern of multilingualism is quite different from the more familiar "transitional" variety. Second, this multilingualism, coupled with the ideals of democracy, puts a serious strain on educational policy and practice, because the needs of each language group have to be met in the curriculum. Third, the neglect of the indigenous languages over a long colonial period clashes with the pressing demand for modernization in a developing country, creating an artificial conflict between the progressivists and the nationalists. Thus the factors of multilingualism, language development, democracy, and modernization interact to produce a complex and tumultuous scene in the area of language policy for education in India. Many of the issues discussed here apply, *mutatis mutandis*, to practically all the multilingual ex-colonial developing countries in Asia and therefore are of comparative significance.

## 2. A LINGUISTIC PROFILE OF INDIA

The complexity of the linguistic scene in India is well known and I shall not rehearse it here. It is necessary, however, to keep in mind certain facts about the geographical distribution, official recognition, actual functions, and relative developmental status of the various languages, in so far as they are relevant to educational language planning.

According to the 1961 census, 1,652 mother tongues were reported in India (Pattanayak 1973). This is not a reliable figure because in some cases the "same" language has been reported under many different names (97 in the case of Hindi) reflecting the respondents' ethnic, professional, attitudinal, regional and other affiliations. Counting only languages reported by more than 1,000 persons and excluding foreign mother tongues, we get approximately 400 languages used in India. These belong to four different language families, namely Indo-Aryan, Dravidian, Sino-Tibetan, and Austro-Asiatic.

Of these, 15 major languages are recognized as "national languages" by the Constitution of India. The following Table includes a list of national languages and the percentage of the total population of India who speak them.

**TABLE 3**

***PERCENTAGE OF SPEAKERS OF THE 15 NATIONAL LANGUAGES OF INDIA****

| Language | % of total population |
|---|---|
| Assamese | 1.63 |
| Bengali | 8.17 |
| Gujarati | 4.72 |
| Hindi | 29.67 |
| Kannada | 3.96 |
| Kashmiri | .44 |
| Malayaḷam | 4.00 |
| Marathi | 7.71 |
| Oriya | 3.62 |
| Punjabi | 3.00 |
| Sanskrit | N |
| Sindhi | .31 |
| Tamil | 6.88 |
| Telugu | 8.17 |
| Urdu | 5.22 |
| Others | 12.50 |

*Based on the 1971 Census (Pattanayak 1977:77)

Speakers of these national languages account for about 87% of the total population of India (about 770 million in 1988).

All of the above languages have rich literary traditions. Some, like Tamil, go back to the beginnings of the Christian era, while

Sanskrit goes back to about 1500 B.C. They are spoken by large segments of the population in well-defined geographical areas (the so-called linguistic states). The exceptions to the geographical distribution are Sindhi, Urdu, and Sanskrit. Sanskrit is not spoken any more for ordinary purposes, but it is an important part of pan-Indian cultural heritage. Sindhi and Urdu are ethnic languages whose speakers are distributed throughout India.

In addition, the Constitution recognizes Hindi as the official language, and English as the associate official language, the latter to be phased out eventually.

Table 3 shows that no single mother-tongue emerges as the dominant majority language of the country. Even Hindi-Urdu, the single largest group, is a minority language in the national context. Thus, India is a nation of linguistic minorities.

The geographic distribution of languages reveals interesting complexities. First of all, proficient use of Hindi-Urdu is largely confined to the north of India, although it is claimed that some form of pidginized Hindi-Urdu is used and understood throughout the country, especially in urban areas. Second, while it is true that most of the states in the country have one dominant language spoken in the region, it is equally true that every state and every district is multilingual (see India Literacy Atlas, 1978). Thus, the claim that speakers of the major national languages account for 87% of the population is slightly misleading if it suggests linguistic homogeneity at the state level and heterogeneity only at the national level. The fact is, not all speakers of a given language are concentrated in their linguistic provinces; sizeable numbers are spread out throughout the nation forming linguistic minorities in their host states. If we exclude the speakers of national languages who do not live in their home states, only about 74% of the total population are mother-tongue speakers of the official language of their home states. Finally, there are a number of languages not listed as national languages in the Constitution. Many of these (around 400) are tribal languages which are not written down (e.g., Gondi, Badaga, etc.). Some others are literary languages whose speakers are either distributed over several states (e.g., Konkani), or do not form the dominant language group in the region (e.g., Tulu in Karnataka), or are foreign languages spoken in border areas (e.g., Nepali) or in erstwhile colonies (e.g., French and Portuguese in Pondicherry and Goa, respectively). These languages are usually referred to by the term "minority languages", although, as we have seen, all languages in India are minority languages. The speakers of these minority languages together with the "migrant" speakers of the national languages constitute a sizeable linguistic minority of 143,667,667 i.e., approximately 26.28% of the then total population of India (Chakledar 1981).

Thus the linguistic profile of India consists of the official language of the country, Hindi; the associate official language used by the educated population throughout the country, English; the 15 national languages recognized by the Constitution, most of which are also dominant state languages; and a number of minority languages, tribal and non-tribal, not given official status by the Constitution.

## 3. LANGUAGES FOR EDUCATION

From the point of view of education, we need to recognize the following typology of languages in India: (1) the classical languages; (2) the regional languages; (3) the mother tongues other than the regional languages; (4) English; and (5) Hindi.

The classical languages are Sanskrit, Persian, and Arabic. Sanskrit is the language of the Hindu scriptures, the epics, classical literature and scientific writing in every field from astronomy to surgery. It was thus the lingua franca of the educated elite, the Pan-Indian vehicle of what has been referred to as "the Great Tradition" (see Basham 1954, 1975). The Muslim invasions and occupations did not replace Sanskrit but added two more classical languages, Persian and Arabic. Persian also enjoyed royal patronage during the Moghul period as the court language. Schools imparting traditional knowledge in these languages flourished all over India and were patronized by the upper, middle, and priestly classes until this "Oriental" tradition was relegated to the background by the "Anglicists" in the nineteenth century. However, they are still in existence all over India, and may be enjoying something of a revival.

The term "regional language" is used to refer to 12 of the 15 "national" languages recognized by the Constitution (i.e., all except Sanskrit, Sindhi, and Urdu). These languages share several important characteristics: (1) they are spoken by large numbers of people; (2) they are spoken in compact geographical areas--in fact, this was the basis of the "reorganization" of states on linguistic lines in 1956, such that each of these languages is the major language of a state (Hindi is the major language of what are now six states); (3) they are also the official languages in their respective states (except Kashmiri in Jammu and Kashmir, where Urdu, the ethnic identity symbol of the predominantly Muslim population, is the official language); (4) most important of all, each of these languages has a long and rich literary tradition, with grammars, writing systems, and recognized standard varieties (see Krishnamurti 1979a). The literature in these languages is rich in what is sometimes called "expressive culture" (i.e., creative writing - prose, poetry, drama, etc.) but lacking in "progressive culture", i.e., the literature of modern empirical science and technology, see Krishnamurti and Mukherji 1985, S. N. Sridhar 1987b). The fact that they are "developed" and "underdeveloped" in different spheres, as we shall see, plays a crucial role in educational planning in modern India.

The third category of languages is what was referred to earlier as minority languages. In each state, there are several types of minorities who speak languages other than the state language. First, there are substantial numbers of migrants from neighboring states; second, there are speakers of unwritten "tribal" languages (these speakers depend on the speakers of the dominant regional language for economic survival, a factor of great significance for education); third, there are speakers of languages which may be neither tribal nor the majority languages, e.g., Konkani, Tulu, etc., and which do not have a script of their own, though many have literature written in the major script of the region; finally, there are members of religious, ethnic, and other minorities who preserve their language, such as the Urdu-speaking Muslims, Sindhi speaking Sindhis all over India, Tamil speaking Iyengars and Telugu speaking Vaishyas in Karnataka. Educationally, the most serious problems are faced by children of those minority groups whose languages lack either a script or a literary tradition.

Next, English is in a category by itself. It is learnt as a subject by most students who cross the elementary stage. It is used as a medium of instruction in most subjects at the university level, and is available as an optional medium at the lower levels. There is a flourishing private industry purporting to educate children through the English medium from the earliest stage. English is still used widely in national and state-level administration, in the mass media, and in inter-regional trade, commerce, higher education, academic exchange, tourism, and other activities.

Hindi, as the official language of the country, is promoted by the Central government in a number of ways. Despite initial resistance, and continued partial boycotting, it continues to spread among the non-Hindi states (see S. N. Sridhar 1987a).

Historically, English replaced Sanskrit as the Pan-Indian language of the learned elite. (Sanskrit had already been weakened in this role by the incursions of Persian.) In the glosso-politics of the country, therefore, one can identify several types of language conflicts or rivalries: (1) English versus the regional languages in the field of education; (2) English versus Hindi for the status of the country's official language and/or lingua franca; (3) one regional language versus another, especially with reference to migrants, as in the case of, e.g., Bengali vs. Assamese in Assam, Tamil vs. Kannada in Karnataka; and (4) the regional languages versus the local (minority) languages at the sub-regional level in the fields of education and administration, e.g., Hindi vs. Maithili in Bihar. At each level, rival language groups are interested in preserving current functions for their language or in acquiring new functions (Annamalai 1979, Khubchandani 1983). In order to understand how the current allocation of roles came about, and to gain insights into substantive synchronic issues (such as the alleged "undeveloped" state of many languages), it is useful to discuss briefly the educational language policy adopted by the British rulers during the colonial era.

## 4. LANGUAGE POLICY IN THE COLONIAL ERA

During the early part of the colonial period, the foreign powers paid little systematic attention to education. Portuguese, Dutch, and French missions established schools in the 16th century, while the British missionaries, who first arrived in 1614, ran schools for Europeans, Anglo-Indians, and certain Indian employees of the East India Company in its major garrison and factory towns.

When the East India Company became a political and administrative power in 1765, it saw political expediency in downplaying the proselytising role of its missionary schools, and established colleges for Muslims and Hindus in 1784 and 1791 respectively. However, it was not until the Charter Act of 1813 that the Company assumed direct responsibility for educating Indians and allocated resources for

> the revival and improvement of literature and encouragement of the learned natives of India and for the introduction of and promotion of the knowledge of science among the inhabitants of the British territories in India. (Sharp 1920:22)

This act was important for two separate reasons: (1) it directed the company to provide facilities for missionaries "to spread useful knowledge and to effect moral improvement" and (2) it inaugurated a state system of education. Both these actions had a tremendous impact on the role of languages in education.

The missionaries played an important role in the study of many Indian languages, especially the less cultivated ones. They started elementary schools where Indian languages were used as media, they wrote the first grammars and textbooks and adapted orthographies for several languages, and edited and translated literary works from others. Their role in promoting English education, however, was far more influential. The schools they established--the "mission schools" and "convents"--where English was the medium of instruction were highly regarded and patronized by progressive, affluent, upwardly mobile Indians, who saw them as conduits to respectable government employment.

**Language in Education**

When the British administration assumed responsibility for educating Indians, it was confronted with the controversial choice between the existing Oriental system and the English system of education. The General Committee of Public Instruction, formed in 1823, was divided between the Orientalists, who advocated the preservation and promotion of Oriental institutions through Persian, Arabic, and Sanskrit, and the Anglicists, who wanted to adopt European style institutions and curriculum (Nurullah and Naik 1964).

The Anglicists were supported by an influential group of Indian social reformers led by Raja Ram Mohun Roy, who were themselves beneficiaries of English education. They knew that English was the key to advancement in the colonial setup. Moreover, they thought of English as a liberating influence against ignorance and superstition, which had kept India in the dark ages. They also genuinely admired the scientific and technological progress of Europe and wished to help Indians partake of it.

The Anglicists' advocacy of English education was based on altogether different motives. They did not disguise their contempt for the native languages and literatures. They espoused an elitist, two-tiered approach to education, whose goal was defined as the creation, in the words of Macaulay's famous Minute, of

> a class of persons Indian in blood and colour, but English in tastes, in opinions, in morals and in intellect. To that class we may leave it to refine the vernacular dialects of the country, to enrich those dialects with terms of science borrowed from the Western nomenclature, and to render them by degrees fit vehicles for conveying knowledge to the great mass of population (Sharp 1920: Document 30).

It is important to remember that the "vernacular dialects" referred to in the Minute included what are now referred to as the 'regional' or the literary languages. The decision to ignore the "vernaculars", and to concentrate on English was a turning point in Indian education, and the current controversy regarding the suitability and readiness of Indian languages to serve as media of science and technology can be traced directly to this decision.

Macaulay's Minute was passed by the British Parliament in 1835, and the then Governor General Lord William Bentick declared that,

> the great object of the British Government ought to be the promotion of European literature and science among the natives of India and that all the funds appropriated

> for the purpose of education would be best employed on English education alone. (Sharp 1920: Document 30)

Subsequent decisions to replace Persian with English as the court language (1837), to give preference in government employment "to those who are educated in English schools" (1844), and the establishment of the three major universities in Bombay, Calcutta, and Madras in 1857 with English as the sole medium of instruction, consolidated the supremacy of English. From this period on, education came to be equated with English education, and those who studied in the Oriental systems were permanently relegated to the background (McCulley 1940:176).

Macaulay's Minute espoused a selective, elitist approach to education; it ignored the education of the "masses" and rejected the native languages. A more liberal and rational policy was promulgated in the "Despatch" of 1854 by the then Governor General, Sir Charles Wood. This "Wood's Despatch" attempted to allocate complementary roles to English and the vernaculars, declaring that,

> In any general system of education, the English language should be taught where there is a demand for it; but such instruction should always be combined with careful attention to the study of the vernacular languages of the district, and with such general instruction as can be conveyed through that language. And while the English language continues to be made use of, as by far the most perfect medium for the education of those persons who have acquired a sufficient knowledge of it to receive general instruction through it, the vernacular language must be employed to teach the far larger classes who are ignorant of, or imperfectly acquainted with English. . . . we look, therefore, to the English language and to the vernacular languages of India together as the media for the diffusion of European knowledge, and it is our desire to see them cultivated together in all schools in India of a sufficiently high class to maintain a school master possessing the requisite qualifications . . . (Bhatt and Aggarwal 1969:8).

Despite the clear role which Wood assigned to the "vernaculars", the emphasis on English continued unabated. The vernaculars were taught only at the elementary level and could be omitted altogether if the pupil so desired.

The sad state of vernacular language eduction did not go unnoticed by the Sadler Commission (1872) and the Education

Commission (1902) appointed by the government to look into the functioning of the universities. The Sadler report noted,

> We are emphatically of opinion that there is something unsound in a system of education which leaves a young man, at the conclusion of his course, unable to speak or write his own mother-tongue fluently and correctly. It is thus beyond controversy that a systematic effort must henceforth be made to promote the serious study of the vernaculars in the secondary schools, intermediate colleges and in the university. . . . (Kanungo 1962:48).

It recommended the use of the vernaculars in the primary and secondary stages, while advocating retention of English as the medium of instruction for all subjects, except the classical and vernacular languages. Although these recommendations resulted in the introduction of the vernacular as compulsory or optional subjects in some universities, such as the Universities of Calcutta and Madras, English continued to occupy its privileged place due to several factors: secondary schools were viewed as preparation for the English medium study at the university stage; knowledge of English was valued as a tool of advancement; English was a safe, neutral choice in multilingual and multidialectal regions; and there was a perceived lack of registers, materials, and teachers in the local languages.

Even the appointment of Indian ministers to the Department of Education in 1921 did not bring about significant change in the situation, since both the socioeconomic reality of the value of English education and the inertia of the educational establishment impeded the change of medium at the university level. Only at the secondary stage, and only in some areas was there a switchover to the regional languages. Thus, the language situation in the Indian educational system during the last decades of colonial rule involved three types of arrangements:

(1) English medium in urban centers for the education of the elite, right from the primary stage;

(2) Two-tier media: vernacular medium for primary stage and English medium for advanced stage;

(3) Vernacular medium in rural areas for primary education (cf. Khubchandani 1983).

Thus, the language policy in education during the colonial era created two dichotomies: first, a dichotomy between the traditional ("Oriental") system of learning and the Western style of education, with emphasis on European (British) literature, empirical science and technology; second, a dichotomy between English medium education and vernacular medium education, with the balance of power resting squarely with the products of the former system. As with other colonial decisions, it is hard to judge whether the language policy was in the interests of the colonizers or the colonized. To the extent that it exposed even a small number of Indians to Western knowledge, it was "progressive"; in so far as this was accomplished at the expense of the indigenous languages, and created an undesirable gap between 'the elite' and the 'masses', it was retrogressive.

## 5. LANGUAGE IN EDUCATION POLICY SINCE INDEPENDENCE

India's independence from British rule in 1947 brought about a number of fundamental changes in language policy. While the language policies during the colonial period dealt essentially with the role of English vis-a-vis the "vernacular" languages, the mandated use of Hindi as the official language brought a new participant into the picture: the constitutional safeguards given to linguistic minorities (though they were only recommendatory and not directive) added yet another element to be reckoned with in formulating a language-in-education policy.

Complicating this task was the federal structure of government adopted in the Constitution, which designated education as a "State" (not federal) subject. The Central government had the role of coordinating the State policies with a view to evolving a national consensus. To this end, the Central government appointed a series of expert committees and commissions whose recommendations were debated, passionately and often violently, in the public forums. The most important of these commissions and their major recommendations are summarized below (India 1953, 1959, Kothari 1970):

(1) The Conference of the Vice Chancellors of Universities (1948), recommended the replacement of English by Indian languages (primarily the major regional languages) as the medium of instruction at the university level within (the unrealistically short period of) five years. (It is interesting to note that this goal has not been achieved even 40 years after the recommendation was made--so much for the effectiveness of committees.)

(2) The Conference of the Education Ministers of the States (1948), recommended the adoption of the mother tongue as the medium of instruction at the primary and secondary school levels, with the state language when it differed from the mother tongue to be studied as a compulsory subject.

(3) The University Education Commission (1949) recommended that students at the secondary and university levels should know three languages, namely the regional language, the link language Hindi, and English.

(4) The Secondary Education Commission (known as the Mudaliar Commission, after its chairman) (1952), endorsed the recommendation of the education ministers' conference and additionally, it recommended the study of at least two other languages, e.g., Hindi and English, at the higher primary level (grades 5 through 8).

(5) The English Review Committee (known after its chairman as the Kunzru committee, appointed by the University Grants Commission in 1955) emphasized the need to "go slow" on the switch over to regional languages as media of instruction at the university level, and urged the need for the continued study of English by all university students even after the switch in the media.

(6) The Central Advisory Board of Education (1957), suggested what has come to be known as the Three Language Formula, which was adopted by the Conference of State Chief Ministers in 1961. This policy recommended the study of (i) the regional language, (ii) Hindi in non-Hindi areas and any other Indian language in the Hindi area, and (iii) English or any other modern European language.

(7) The Education Commission (also known as the Kothari Commission, after its chairman) (1964-1966), looked into the problems faced by the states in implementing the Three Language Formula, and recommended a "modified, graduated" Three Language Formula, which won general (though by no means unanimous, see below) acceptance. This is the language policy currently in force in most of India. (For a more detailed discussion, see K. Sridhar 1977).

## 5.1 Number and Choice of Languages to Study: The Three Language Formula

The Three Language Formula is a compromise between the demands of the various pressure groups and has been hailed as a masterly--if imperfect--solution to a complicated problem. It seeks to accommodate the interests of group identity (mother tongues and regional languages), national pride and unity (Hindi), administrative efficiency and technological progress (English). It also seeks flexibility by mandating compulsory status to some languages and optional status for the study of others, by prescribing the order of introduction and length of study, as well as by making available different choices in different linguistic regions (e.g., the Hindi vs. non-Hindi areas), all within a uniform overall framework. This complicated series of choices, as summarized by Nadkarni (1977:101), is given in Table 4 and will be briefly discussed.

According to the Formula, the child is required to study one language at the lower primary stage (grades 1-4), two languages at the higher primary level (grades 5-7), three languages at the lower secondary level (grades 8-10), two languages at the higher secondary level (grades 11-12). No language is obligatory at the university level.

**TABLE 4**

***Modified and Graduated Three Language Formula***

| Educational level | | | Languages as subjects of study |
|---|---|---|---|
| Lower Primary (Classes I-IV) | | | Mother tongue (Regional Language) |
| Higher Primary (Classes V-VIII) | | (1) | Mother tongue (Regional Language) |
| | | (2) | English |
| Lower Secondary (Classes VIII-X) | | (1) | Mother tongue (Regional Language) |
| | | (2) | Hindi in non-Hindi areas and a modern Indian Language in Hindi areas |
| | | (3) | English |
| Higher Secondary | | | Any two from Group A or Group B |
| | (A) | (1) | Mother tongue (Regional Language) |
| | | (2) | Hindi in non-Hindi areas and a modern Indian Language in Hindi area |
| | | (3) | English |
| | (B) | (1) | A modern Indian language |
| | | (2) | A modern foreign language |
| | | (3) | A classical language, Indian or foreign |
| University | | | No language compulsory |

As for the choice of languages, the Formula provides a certain degree of flexibility. At the lower primary level, children whose mother tongue is the official language of the state (the case with about 74% of India's population) study that language. Children who speak languages which are a minority in their region can in most cases study their mother tongue; others study the regional language. (The current policy is to arrange for the teaching of a minority mother tongue if there are at least 10 students in a given grade level requesting it. The higher one goes up the grade levels, the more limited the facilities for learning the minority mother tongue become, especially in the case of speakers of languages other than the national languages).

At the higher primary level (grades 5-7), students begin to learn a compulsory second language. In the Hindi areas this is usually English. In the non-Hindi areas also, the preferred choice is English, though the formula permits the choice of Hindi at this level. In addition to this second compulsory language, students may optionally add another language at this level--English or Hindi, whichever was not chosen as the compulsory language.

At the lower secondary stage (grades 8-10) a third compulsory language is introduced. At this stage, students in the non-Hindi areas begin learning Hindi and continue their study of English and the mother tongue or regional language. Students in the Hindi areas are supposed to add a modern Indian language, though they in fact choose a classical language such as Sanskrit, Persian, or Arabic or choose some other option.

At the higher secondary stage (grades 11-12), students may continue to study any two of the languages studied so far (i.e., mother tongue and English) or they may learn any two of the following: a modern Indian language (e.g., Marathi), a classical language (e.g., Sanskrit), or a modern foreign language (e.g., French).

### 5.1.1 *Problems of Interpretation and Implementation*

Though the Three Language Formula is generally regarded as the least unacceptable of all the policies proposed so far, it has been interpreted and implemented differently in different parts of the country. Two states, Tamil Nadu in the South and Mizoram in the East, have refused to accept it, and follow a Two Language Policy (Mother tongue/regional language and English) instead. In some non-Hindi states, (for example, West Bengal and Orissa) the classical language Sanskrit is taught in place of Hindi as the third language. In certain other non-Hindi states, students are required to take courses in Hindi but need not pass them, or the passing mark is fixed at a very low level. Many Hindi states are less than enthusiastic about teaching a (non-Hindi related) modern Indian language as the third language, as the Education Commission had suggested they would in the hope of promoting national integration (Report of the Education Commission 1964-66:59). Instead, they tend to teach Sanskrit (which, being the "parent" of modern Indo-Aryan languages of North India, is presumably easier to learn) or Persian or Arabic or another Indo-Aryan language of the North, e.g., Marathi or Bengali. This creates resentment, especially in the Southern states, where the genetically unrelated Dravidian languages are spoken. The South Indians feel that the formula "imposes" a "North Indian" language on them, while the North Indians are not made to learn a South Indian language. The fact that the language policies implemented in the Hindi areas is a reflection of the sociolinguistic status of Hindi vis-a-vis the South Indian languages is, of course, of no consolation to the critics of this policy. However, despite an occasional flurry of protests in the form of letters to editors and sporadic political speeches, the Three Language Formula seems to have come to stay in India. The Central Government has (wisely) kept a low profile in the controversy, appearing to promote all languages, continuing its munificent patronage of Hindi, and slowly but surely introducing Hindi, without dislodging English, into more and more domains in the administration (see Dwivedi 1981). Thus, the real growth of Hindi in its role as the official language of the country has had the effect of softening up the opposition. If anything, more and more people see an advantage in knowing Hindi (see S. N. Sridhar 1987a).

A major problem with the Three Language Formula lies in its treatment of children belonging to the linguistic minorities (whether because of migration, tribal affiliation, or small numbers in their state of residence), who are faced with the cruel choice of either learning four languages or foregoing their mother tongue: they need the regional language for all practical, administrative, and academic purposes at the higher grade levels. In many urban centers, there are schools, government and private, which impart education through Grade 10 in certain minority languages. In such schools, students can theoretically study only three languages (mother tongue, Hindi, and English, for example). However, such facilities are available only in large cities and towns, and only for the children of migrants who speak one of the major national languages or the official language of a neighbor state. Even in those schools, there is increasing pressure to make the teaching of the regional language compulsory. Thus we come back to the four language plan. As for the minorities who do not speak one of the major regional languages (about 13% of the population), they are forced to learn the local regional language in addition to their mother tongue around grade level of 5 or so, (since higher education is, in most cases, available only through the major language of the region) or English, at a later stage.

Thus the Three Language Formula seeks to solve the problem of the number of languages to be studied in a multilingual country by accommodating the regional language, the language of higher education, and the official language, at the expense of the classical language and the minority mother tongue. Of course, students can and do study these other languages as optional languages, but this adds more languages to a curriculum already heavily skewed in favor of languages as opposed to other subjects.

Another aspect of this solution is worth noting. While the Formula makes it possible for a citizen to acquire the languages needed to perform most of the highly valued functions, it does pose an extra burden on the 26% of the population who speak the "minority" languages. Thus, even in a democracy, multilingualism has not been accommodated without some cost to the linguistic minorities although the present structure gives the regional languages their rightful place in education.

## 5.2 Medium of Instruction

The second major language issue in Indian education is the choice of the medium of instruction at various levels and in different fields. It is here that the debate about language development becomes acute.

There are two chief questions relating to the medium of teaching: (1) what should be the medium of minority language speakers at the early stage? and (2) how long should English continue to be the medium at the university stage?

The government of India, as well as all the state governments, subscribe to the principle of using the mother tongue as the medium of instruction at least in the initial stages, ideally throughout the educational career. In the case of speakers of the major national languages of the country (covering approximately 87% of the population), there has been no serious problem in implementing this policy, except in small towns and rural areas where teachers may not be available for small numbers of children of migrants. The real problem is the choice of medium of instruction for the minorities who speak one of the unrecognized (tribal or other) languages. Many of these languages are (i) not cultivated, (ii) do not enjoy official recognition for administrative purposes. Therefore, the main reason for using them as subjects and/or media is to affirm the student's linguistic identity and to aid the learning of basic skills such as literacy, and arithmetic. Beyond this stage, it is felt that many of these languages are of little practical value to the child, if only because there is little written material available in these languages.

### 5.2.1 *Tribal Languages in Education: A Survey of Teacher Attitudes*

In this connection, it may be of interest to examine some empirical evidence on attitudes to the teaching of tribal languages. The evidence comes from a pilot survey of teacher attitudes to the teaching of tribal languages vis-a-vis other languages, conducted by the present author in Bihar during the Summer of 1987. According to the 1981 census, Bihar (with Orissa), has the third largest concentration of tribal populations in India (5.9 million each) after Madhya Pradesh (12 million).

The survey was done by means of a questionnaire given to 56 faculty members teaching in schools and colleges in various towns and cities in Bihar: e.g., Ranchi, Chas, Dhanbad, Lohardagga and Jhumritillaya. In some cases, questionnaires were followed with interviews. Of the 56 faculty members who participated in the survey, 89% claimed Hindi as their mother tongue, while 47% claimed bilingualism in Hindi and a tribal language (as their mother tongue). The analysis reveals that most of the respondents are highly qualified, with 91% possessing degrees, bachelors and beyond.

| | |
|---|---|
| Ph.D. | 12.5% |
| MA/M.Sc./M.Com. | 46.4% |
| BA/B.Sc./B.Com. | 32.1% |
| Matriculation | 9.0% |

About 45% of the faculty members stated that they had students from various minority language backgrounds. The languages reported are Oraon, Mundari, Kurux, Kharia, Ho, and Adivasi. The next question asked if the faculty were given any choice in choosing the language of instruction. The respondents claimed that they were given a choice and that 93% had chosen Hindi as the medium. The reasons for the choice become apparent in response to the question that follows. When asked about the language their students felt most comfortable in, Hindi was chosen by 95% of the respondents. Thus, for tribal speakers, the regional language Hindi is preferable to their Mother Tongue or English. Asked if tribal languages should be taught in schools, slightly more than half of them, 64.3%, responded in the affirmative, while 35.7% responded in the negative. When probed further, and asked if parents demand that tribal languages be taught, 73.2% said "Yes" and 26.8% said "No". The next two questions were intended to further explore the issue of teaching tribal languages. The data indicates that the respondents were divided. Asked if qualified teachers were easy to find to teach tribal languages, 48.2% said it was easy, 35.7%,said it was difficult, and 16.1% did not answer the question. On the question of the scope for the use of these languages outside the classroom, 54.1% felt there was scope, 45.8% felt there was none.

Some who responded in the affirmative qualified their statement with a short note, stating that qualified teachers were available only for primary grades, and that the tribal languages should be taught to promote regional/cultural development.

The next two questions were related to the three language formula. Asked if the "three language formula" was necessary, and to explain "which three languages should be studied and why" the respondents were unanimous in their support for the three language formula. The choice of the three languages and reasons for studying them are given in Table 5. The specific choices and reasons listed are the respondents' own, not suggested by the researcher. Some respondents wrote more than one response, hence the figures do not add up to 100%.

**TABLE 5**

*Reasons for Studying Various Languages, According to Teachers*

| | |
|---|---|
| *English* should be studied because it is: | |
| an international language | 67.8% |
| language of tourism | 16.1% |
| language of higher education | 7.1% |
| an easy and concise language | 11.1% |
| *Hindi* should be studied because it is: | |
| our national language and for national integration | 58.9% |
| our mother tongue | 26.8% |
| easy to understand/our language | 7.1% |
| *Tribal* languages should be studied: | |
| for regional/cultural development | 73.2% |
| only in the primary stages | 26.8% |

The respondents were well aware of the realities, and their choices in the above question are further substantiated in their response to the following question: "What level of competence should be expected in each of the above languages?" The overall consensus was:

| | |
|---|---|
| Hindi: | full command: understand, speak, read, write |
| English: | only read and write |
| Tribal: | understand and speak |

The data, though limited and informally collected, underscores an important point. Ekka (1984) claims that the reasons for the non-use of tribal languages in education is due to lack of commitment on the part of the authorities. My data suggests that it is the economic and cultural pressure that is forcing the tribal languages to perform mostly "L" functions (Ferguson 1959).

The policy, therefore, has been to provide two types of schools: (i) where the "principal" medium is the official language of the state (the majority of schools are of this type) and (ii) where a minority language is used as the medium of instruction whenever there are at least 10 students in a given class who request it. In the case of the so-called "uncultivated" or tribal languages, they are used as media usually only up to the end of the primary grades (hence referred to as "subordinate" media) at which point the state languages take their place as the chief medium. This may be referred to as "mainstreaming". When the minority language is one of the recognized national languages (e.g., Kannada in Andhra Pradesh), it is allowed to be used throughout the school years.

It is obvious that compared to the number of mother tongues, the number of languages taught as subjects or media is small. According to the Third All-India Educational Survey (1981), at present 58 languages are studied and used as media of instruction in the states and union territories. The languages (cultivated or tribal) and their roles (as first, second or third) are as follows. The following 21 languages are cultivated literary languages (with the exception of Khasi and Mizo) and are also recognized official languages, and are used as first, second or third languages: Arabic, Assamese, Bengali, English, French, Gujarati, Hindi, Kannada, Khasi, Konkani, Malayalam, Manipuri, Marathi, Mizo, Oriya, Persian, Punjabi, Sanskrit, Tamil, Telugu, Urdu.

The following 11 languages (most of which are tribal languages, except for Sindhi, Nepali and Tibetan) are either used as media of instruction or are studied as second and third languages. These include: Angami, Ao, Chokri, Garo, Karen, Konyak, Lotha, Nepali, Sema, Sindhi, Tibetan.

The remaining 26 languages are studied only as subjects, as second or third languages. None are used as media of instruction. These are: Bodhi, Bodo, Chakma, Ghang, Dogri, German, Hmar, Kashmiri, Khezha, Khiemnunger, Kuki, Lai, Lakher, Latin, Nicobaree,

Pali, Pawi, Phom, Portuguese, Rengma, Sangatam, Santhali, Syriac, Tripuri, Yimchunger, Zeliang (Chaturvedi and Singh 1981:37-38).

We have so far discussed the medium at the school level. Replacing English as the medium of instruction at the university level has proved to be more problematic. Many of the reasons for this situation are common to many multilingual formerly colonial nations: the value of English as a "neutral" language among rival native languages; the nation-wide and international acceptability of English compared to the territorial restriction imposed by the regional languages; the lack of vocabulary and registers in the regional languages in the areas of science, engineering, medicine, etc.; the fear of provincialization and retrogression in an age of rapid mobility and technological innovations; above all, the delay in giving official recognition to the regional languages in such domains as administration, and law, and the consequent perception of the limited value of regional language education. This phenomenon is fairly obvious when one looks at the number of candidates who opted to write their Indian Administrative Service examinations in the language of their choice. For the periods 1982 to 1983 (the periods for which data is available), few candidates exercised their language rights. The total number of candidates who appeared at the examination with an Indian language as an optional subject was as follows: Paper I: 633, Paper II: 630 in 1982; Paper I: 855, Paper II: 848 in 1983. Percentage of such candidates in relation to the total number of candidates who appeared at the examination are 7.32% and 7.29% in 1982, and 9.16% and 9.08% in 1983, respectively. (Sharma 1985: 39)

### 5.2.2 *Efforts Toward Language Development*

The educational planning agencies--the Central and State governments, the University Grants Commission, the universities and training colleges have taken a number of steps to answer the critics of regional language media and to facilitate the process of switch-over. They point out that a language "develops" only when put to new uses; nevertheless, attempts are made to hasten the process by creating technical terms for use in textbooks and class rooms. Generous subsidies are given to state education departments to commission textbooks in various subjects in regional languages. The state governments and universities, in turn, have opened either colleges where the exclusive medium is the regional language, or sections of courses are taught in the regional languages.

These efforts have also been criticized on various grounds. The central government sought to remedy the fear of provincialization by offering a grant of about one million dollars each to states using textbooks written using the "standard" (Pan-Indian) terminology suggested by its Directorate of Terminology. However, the new technical terms have been criticized as strange and unnatural, having been coined by purists from Sanskrit roots and often involving unpronounceable clusters--in short, the new terms are as opaque as the English ones they are meant to replace, without the latter's advantage of international currency. The style in which the new textbooks are written has also been criticized as stilted because of direct translation of English syntactic patterns.

In this context, the suggestion made by Krishnamurti (1979a) seems to be eminently practical. He recommends that the teachers of science subjects should take a pragmatic approach to the problem of terminology. Without worrying too much about language purity, they should employ whatever technical terms come naturally to them in the course of teaching in the regional languages--in other words, resort to extensive code switching and code mixing. Over years of use, a terminology adapted to the situational context will naturally evolve from practice.

Quite apart from the problem of terminology there are problems with the production and distribution of regional language textbooks (Naik 1980). Gupta (1980:97-99) cites several cases of inefficiency all around to illustrate the poor show of regional language textbooks at the university level. The Telugu Academy of Andhra Pradesh translated *Advanced Accounts* by Shukla and Grewal into Telugu and marketed this book in two volumes at the subsidized price of Rs.78, as compared to Rs.35 of the original English language edition. The result was that only 929 copies of Volume I and 639 copies of Volume II were sold between 1973/74 and 1976/77, whereas about 30,000 copies of the English edition are sold every year. This is equally true of other regional language textbooks. Several books published between 1970-1977 in Bengali for students in West Bengal received a similar fate (Gupta 1980:98).

### 5.2.3. *Medium of Instruction at the Universities: The Current Scene*

Despite the problems noted above, universities seem to be making a steady, if slow, progress toward Indianizing the medium of instruction. The recent (1981) statistics on the medium of instruction in Indian universities in various subject areas and at the graduate and undergraduate levels are given in Table 6 below. (The statistics in this table were compiled by the present author from the figures published in the Universities Handbook 1981-82.) It is clear from this Table that English is still (the figures are for 1981) pervasive in the university system. Even so the regional languages have entered the picture as optional, alternative media--though they are clearly not as popular among students, especially in the science and the professional courses, and especially at the graduate level. There are very few universities which offer instruction exclusively through the regional language, and all of these are in the Hindi area. The hegemony of English is even more pronounced at specialized institutions such as the agricultural universities, the prestigious Indian Institutes of Technology and a number of institutions of higher learning such as the Indian Management Institute and the so-called "deemed universities".

**TABLE 6**

***Medium of Instruction at Graduate and Postgraduate Levels for Different Courses at Indian Universities***

| Subject | Level | Regional Language | English | Regional Language and English | Other |
|---|---|---|---|---|---|
| Arts | Ugr. | 12 | 16 | 50 | 9 |
| | Gr. | 6 | 43 | 33 | 5 |
| Science | Ugr. | 10 | 23 | 43 | 13 |
| | Gr. | 3 | 58 | 21 | 7 |
| Commerce | Ugr. | 11 | 15 | 48 | 15 |
| | Gr. | 5 | 37 | 26 | 19 |
| Law | Ugr. | 4 | 41 | 26 | 3 |
| | Gr. | 0 | 30 | 12 | 3 |
| Engineering | Ugr. | 1 | 48 | 3 | 37 |
| | Gr. | 0 | 37 | 3 | 49 |
| Medicine | Ugr. | 0 | 53 | 5 | 2 |
| | Gr. | 0 | 48 | 4 | 3 |

(Based on *Universities Handbook* 1981-1982:1245-1249).

Although it is encouraging to note that so many universities offer the regional languages as additional or alternative media, the reality is less rosy than the statistics. For, the two alternatives are not valued equally. Often the regional language media classes have very few students. Unfortunately, the enrollment figures for the regional language sections vis-a-vis English are not available. Observations show that the former are not popular. Students have to be coaxed to enter the regional language medium courses.

Alternatively, lack of proficiency in English is used as a device to fill the regional language medium classes. Though the empirical evidence is not available on this point, in general, there is a perception that these courses are chosen by the less academically ambitious students.

The main reason for the less than enthusiastic response from students and parents to the regional language medium is attitudinal. English is (correctly) perceived as potentially more useful--a larger number of more highly valued roles are made possible by the study of English (see chapter 7). One such role is nation-wide mobility, which even Hindi does not provide. Another is entry into elite institutions of higher learning, such as the Indian Management Institute and the Indian Institutes of Technology. A third is perceived (and probably real) advantage in all-India competitive examinations for prestigious civil service executive positions, such as the Indian Administrative Service. Yet another is the opportunity to go abroad for higher study. Finally, there is the greater relative prestige in society which manifests itself in many ways, e.g., higher paying jobs, a more expeditious response from government and business employers, etc.

The second major reason, which complements the higher evaluation of English, is the (still) widespread belief that the regional languages are simply not yet ready to function as media for technical subjects, despite the assurance of the experts. While the value of mother tongue medium is readily conceded, those who can afford to (including the most militant protagonists of the regional languages) send their children to (private) English medium schools and colleges.

The official policy of encouraging the regional languages, often at the expense of English, has had at least two potentially serious consequences: (i) it has resulted in the flight of the urban middle classes from the public (government) schools to privately managed English medium schools. The latter have been mushrooming at an alarming rate--alarming because their only qualifications often are the English medium, and the trappings of the missionary schools such as school uniforms: the quality of instruction is not necessarily better. Their attraction is so great that even a lower middle class family thinks nothing of spending a precious part of its income on the high fees charged by such schools rather than patronizing the free government school. (ii) Just as the critics had feared, professional mobility is being curtailed. The principle of hiring the best candidate regardless of which part of the country he/she comes from has had to be compromised because of the requirement that the candidate be able to use the regional language in the work place. Some critics feel that this reduces competition and leads to provincialism.

In a sense, the dilemma of the medium is not unlike the other dilemmas in which the Indian educational institutions find themselves caught. Consider for example the policy of affirmative action toward the traditionally depressed castes. The prevalent mode of implementing this policy, both in education and public employment, has been through a quota system: a certain proportion of "seats" and positions are reserved at each level for candidates from the 'scheduled' castes and tribes and other minorities. But this policy has been subjected to the same criticisms as the language policy. There seems to be no painless solution. The hope is that this is only a short term problem of transition from feudalism/colonialism to democracy.

## 6. CONCLUSION

On the basis of the foregoing discussion, I would like to make the following tentative generalizations concerning the evolution of language policies in education in a multilingual country. To what extent these remarks apply to other countries is an empirical question, whose examination will direct our efforts to evolve theoretical paradigms.

(1) Education in multilingual countries has to provide for a supra-regional language that performs not only the "L" functions of a lingua franca but also the "H" functions in the sense of Ferguson 1959. In fact, the part of the educational policy which concerns the "H" functions will be more successfully implemented than that part which deals with the "L" functions. In India, the widespread variation in the implementation of the provision for Hindi in the Three Language Formula is a case in point, since Hindi still performs relatively few "H" functions compared to English.

(2) In a multilingual democracy, language policies in education evolve in the direction of languages lower on the prestige hierarchy annexing more and more valued roles in the educational system by weakening the exclusive rights of the prestige languages. This point is supported at two stages in the evolution of language policies in India--first, the struggle of the 15 major "national" languages for recognition in the educational system, and now, a similar struggle, being waged by the "minority" languages, for status first as a subject language at the elementary level, then throughout the school system, subsequently as the medium of instruction at the early stages and finally at the university level, in all subjects. This battle is far from complete in India, even for the major languages, and has not yet begun for scores of minority languages.

# Chapter 3

# Sociolinguistic Theory and Non-Native Varieties of English

## 1. INTRODUCTION

This chapter attempts to explore the implications for sociolinguistic theory of "one of the most significant linguistic phenomena of our time, the incredible spread of English as a global language" (Ferguson 1982: vii). From a speech community consisting of about 7 million speakers on a little island at the time of Shakespeare (Quirk 1985), English has spread to every corner of the world, and is used today by over 700 million speakers, out of which nearly or more than half may be non-native users (Strevens 1982).[1] Generations, in some cases centuries, of use in alien socio-cultural contexts has led to the emergence of several non-native varieties of English, including second language varieties, such as Indian English, and foreign language varieties, such as Japanese English.

Although variation has been a central theme in sociolinguistic research of the last three decades, it is only recently that variation in the use of language by non-native speakers has come to be taken seriously in mainstream research. However, among the different types of non-native varieties, only the study of pidgins has received much attention (Hymes 1971). Other types, for example, second and foreign language varieties of languages such as English, have not played a role in the development and testing of sociolinguistic theories (see, for example, the textbooks by Trudgill (1974), Dittmar (1976), Hudson (1980), among others).

By ignoring non-native variation except pidgins the standard textbooks imply that either it does not properly fall in the domain of mainstream sociolinguistic research or that the current models are quite adequate to account for this phenomenon. Both these assumptions need to be reexamined in the light of recent work (see Smith 1981, 1983, Kachru 1982a, and Pride 1982) on non-native varieties of English. In this chapter I will attempt to show that non-native varieties, especially the established 'institutionalized' second language varieties such as Indian English, Singapore English, Filipino English, and Nigerian English, pose, in a particularly focused form, many of the problems with which sociolinguistic theory is concerned. I will argue that a theoretically oriented study of such varieties contributes to a better understanding of concepts such as sociolinguistic typology, macro- and micro- sociolinguistic determinants of variation, the role of functional distribution in the establishment of indigenous norms, the role of socio-cultural factors in language acquisition, and the dynamics of language standardization and language planning, among others.

The reasons why non-native varieties (NNV's hereafter) have not entered the mainstream of sociolinguistic research parallel the reasons for a similar neglect, until recently, of pidgins, Black English, and other "non-standard" varieties. First, dialectologists considered them marginal to the main focus of their studies, namely native varieties. Second, they were denied systematicity, being regarded essentially as a collection of idiosyncratic "errors" or "localisms" caused by indolence or ignorance (Prator 1968, Newmark 1966). Third, even when systematicity was implicitly conceded by discussing the phenomena under such titles as "Indian English: An examination of the errors of idioms made by Indians in writing English" (Whitworth 1907) the approach was prescriptive and corrective rather than descriptive or scientific. Fourth, the negative pedagogical stereotypes were adopted by the speakers of these varieties themselves, who did not think their "corrupt" or "degenerate" renditions were worthy of serious description or codification.

These reasons are interesting from the point of view of the history and sociology of science. The relegation of the NNV's to a marginal status follows from a sacred cow in linguistics namely, the

> special place [given] to the native speaker as the only truly valid and reliable source of language data whether those data are the elicited texts of the descriptivists or the intuitions the theorist works with (Ferguson 1982:vii).

The second reason, denial of the systematicity of the NNV's, is not unlike other manifestations of prejudice which are then used to justify unequal treatment. The pedagogical attitude which insists on conformity with the prescriptive norms, even from the earliest stage of language learning, derives from a long-held axiom in language teaching which has only recently come to be challenged. Finally, the self-annulling attitude of non-native speakers is of course typical of low prestige languages all over the world.

In addition to these axiomatic and attitudinal barriers, there has been a serious, practical obstacle which has come in the way of the desired integration. This is the paucity of detailed, rigorous descriptions of the varieties which either explicitly address or contain data of the sort that can be used to address current issues in sociolinguistic theory. Most of the descriptions are either impressionistic or fragmentary. They present a wealth of individual features attributed to the varieties but are often lacking in crucial background information on the sources of the data, the conditions of elicitation, or the regularity of its occurrence. There is virtually no empirical or experimental evidence as to the relationship between the occurrence of a given feature and the socio-economic, educational, substratum characteristics of the speakers (some exceptions to be discussed later are Kachru 1976, Smith and Rafiqzad 1979, Platt and Weber 1980, Parasher 1980, Shaw 1981, and chapter 7). Because most of the studies of NNV's contain observations which, eminently plausible though they may be, are stated in such broad or vague terms as to need considerable specification before being subjected to empirical validation, the study of NNV's may be said to be still in a pre-theoretical stage. One of the aims of this chapter, therefore, is to make explicit the relationship between some aspects of the descriptive data and current theoretical issues in sociolinguistics. The rest of the chapter is organized as follows. Section 2 deals with sociolinguistic typology: here I will present arguments for treating three types of NNV's--pidgins, indigenized varieties of English (IVE's), and foreign language varieties (FLV's)--as separate sociolinguistic categories defined in terms of explicitly stated criteria. The rest of the chapter will focus on IVE's. Section 3 deals with methodological issues in describing the formal properties of IVE's. Section 4 explores situational features contributing to the distinctiveness of IVE's; section 5 is concerned with selected applied sociolinguistic issues raised by IVE's. The final section 6 brings the discussion together.

## 2. A SOCIOLINGUISTIC TYPOLOGY OF NON-NATIVE VARIETIES

The second language and foreign language varieties have, in a sense, fallen between two stools in sociolinguistic research. At one extreme, they are regarded as "nothing but" pidgins, and at another extreme, they seem to be "varieties" like other native varieties. In order to motivate a separate categorial status in sociolingustic theory for these varieties, it is necessary to differentiate them from pidgins at one end and native varieties at the other, and of course, from each other. I will attempt to do this in this section with reference to a set of explicit criteria based on formal features, functional range, and evaluations of status. I will not compare these varieties to creoles, since they are not *native* languages of the respective communities.

## 2.1 Structural Complexity

Although linguists are not in complete agreement as to the necessary and sufficient features of a pidgin, it is generally conceded that pidgins involve the following characteristics: a drastically reduced vocabulary (as few as 700 to 1,000 words in the case of Sango, see Samarin 1971:119), elimination of several types of grammatical features, and an extremely limited functional range. Attitudinally, they carry very little prestige (Hymes 1971). The other two major types of NNV's are sharply differentiated from pidgins with respect to all these criteria. Taking as our basis the educated varieties of these speech forms (I will turn to the question of how these are defined in Section 3), the following observations can be made about second and foreign language varieties: they show no such "impoverishment" of vocabulary as the pidgins. On the contrary, IVE's exhibit *expansion* in the area of the lexicon. This expansion is effected through several processes including heavy borrowing from the native languages; calques; hybrid words and compounds; novel collocations not attested in native varieties; and neologisms created by the application of regular word-formation rules of the reference language (e.g., "me-and-my-darling" for 'loveseat' in African English, see Kachru 1975, Bokamba 1982). This feature of creativity has been cited by some linguists as a ground for classifying IVE's as 'dialects' of the reference languages on par with native dialects (Halverson 1966). This feature also distinguishes IVE's from the foreign language varieties--the latter tend to be conservative. In the area of grammar, even the middle level sub-varieties ('mesolects,' see Richards 1982) of IVE's are marked by regular differences from the reference language patterns, for example, in embedded questions, invariable tag in tag questions, use of present perfect for simple past, omission of articles, use of mass nouns as count nouns, use of the progressive aspect with verbs of perception, among others (cf. Tay and Gupta 1983, Bokamba 1982, Kachru 1969). While some of these features may be viewed as examples of "simplification" characteristic of pidgins, it is clear that the grammar of IVE's is both quantitatively, and more important, substantively different from that of pidgins. IVE's do not show elimination of grammatical categories such as number, gender, etc., and elimination of redundant features as in pidgins. Their sentence structure is marked by a degree of complexity (measured in terms of, e.g., the range of embeddings, and types of subordinating and coordinating devices employed) comparable to that found in native varieties. The paucity of available research on FLV's makes it difficult to say whether they are different from IVE's in this respect. Observational evidence indicates that they are also marked by grammatical differences from the reference language norms but these differences do not amount to 'reduction' (cf. Stanlaw 1982). However, the question of the nature and degree of formal differences between IVE's and FLV's is an important topic of research that has yet to be addressed adequately.

### 2.2 Functional Range

The three types of IVE's are sharply differentiated in terms of *functional range* also. Traditionally, the functional range of a language has been discussed in the framework of Fishman's (1965) concept of *domains* or institutional contexts, defined in terms of factors such as location, topic, and participants. Typical domains investigated in the literature include family, neighborhood, school, work, religion, transactions such as shopping, and others. Of course, a finer analysis involving different combinations of topic, participants and style is employed to arrive at a detailed profile of the functional range of a language or variety.

Most pidgins are employed in a severely restricted range of domains, e.g., trading, plantations, tourism. (Some pidgins, e.g., Tok Pisin, are now used in an extended range of domains including school and administration, but these are arguably varieties on their way to becoming second languages.) FLV's, on the other hand, are used in a wider range of contexts such as international trade, international scientific and cultural exchange (e.g., conferences), and tourism. It may be noted that all these domains involve contact with speakers of the reference language, whether native or non-native, as in the case of a Korean businessman or scientist interacting with his or her Norwegian or Colombian counterpart. FLV's are rarely used in intranational domains such as in local government offices or among friends discussing everyday topics. (A possible exception may be technical discussions among scientists or engineers.) In contrast, IVE's have a broad functional range. They are typically used in all or most of the following domains: administration, education (as subject language and as medium of instruction) especially at the higher levels, inter-regional communication (involving business people, scientists, engineers and other professionals, as well as in travel and correspondence), in the national and regional media, in general conversations and transactions among the educated people, and in creative writing. This range of intranational use is undoubtedly the single most important factor determining the form and status of IVE's. Convincing empirical support for the typological differences between

IVE's and FLVs posited here may be found in Shaw (1981) discussed in detail later on in this chapter.

### 2.3 Evaluation of Functions

As important as the *range* is the *evaluation* of functions performed by the three types of non-native varieties. The functions of pidgins are typically not highly valued while those of IVE's are analogous to those of the 'High' variety in a diglossic situation (but see section 4 for qualifications). FLV's also perform high functions relative to pidgins but they are not as highly valued across a range of domains. The importance of the evaluation of functions rather than simply the functional range is illustrated by the fact that in India, English is the lingua franca of the educated elites in high domains while Hindi functions as a low level lingua franca (see chapter 7).

### 2.4 Stability, Intelligibility, and Mode of Acquisition

IVE's and foreign language varieties are also unlike pidgins in some other respects. (1) IVE's have time depth. Indian English, for example, has a history of over two centuries, and there is evidence that this variety is actually increasing its uses. (Consider, for example, the tremendous proliferation of popular journals in English all over the country in the last decade). FLV's are also relatively more 'stable' than pidgins. (2) A pidgin is not mutually *intelligible* with the reference language. IVE's and FLV's in their more educated or 'standard' forms are intelligible (Bansal 1969, Nelson 1982, Smith and Rafiqzad 1979). (3) Pidgins are primarily learnt by informal contact. The primary agency for the learning of IVE's and FLV's is through formal instruction. There is, of course, a greater degree of environmental support and hence opportunity for informal learning in IVE's, something that is markedly lacking in the learning of FLV's.

The arguments presented in this section are, I believe, sufficient to motivate the setting up of IVE's and FLV's as separate sociolinguistic types analogous to categories such as geographical and social varieties, pidgins, creoles, and diglossic varieties. I will now examine to what extent the theoretical concepts and methods used in current sociolinguistic models may be applied to the description of these varieties. The discussion will be based primarily on data from Indian English but I will occasionally refer to other IVE's as well.

## 3. PROBLEMS IN THE DESCRIPTION OF INDIGENIZED VARIETIES

Descriptions of second language varieties such as Indian English so far have adopted what may be termed a *deviationist* approach, contrasting the non-native formal patterns with those of British or American English. This approach suffers from two drawbacks. First, the term 'deviation' used by linguists such as Kachru (1969) has been interpreted as a potentially judgmental characteristic (Mehrotra 1982), although it was intended only in a descriptive sense. Second, the contrastive approach has resulted in the listing of a heterogeneous set of departures from the native norms, collectively labelled 'Indian English', 'Filipino English', 'Nigerian English', 'Singapore English', and so forth. An examination of the long lists of features claimed to mark any of the second language varieties reveals that they are based on data gathered from speakers with different levels of proficiency, different mother tongue backgrounds, and different styles of usage. It is not clear that the features in question are representative of the variety at large as the labelling seems to imply. This is, of course, an empirical question, but one that is more relevant in the case of non-native varieties than native ones because of the range of proficiency characteristic of the former. The contrastive approach, therefore, is useful only as an initial stage of analysis to identify the variables. It needs to be supplemented by (a) a *systemic* approach that seeks to explain how the putative features pattern into an autonomous system; and (b) a *sociolinguistic* approach that seeks to predict the social and/or linguistic circumstances in which a given formal feature is likely to occur.

I will briefly discuss this point with selected examples of Indian English. Consider the observation that Indian English speakers tend to use the non-past perfect form where a native speaker would use the simple past (e.g., 'I have gone there yesterday'). This observation is correct (at least of certain mother tongue varieties, e.g., Telugu) but inadequate, unless a complete analysis of the set of aspectual contrasts in Indian English is given in sui generis terms. Similar analyses are needed to illuminate the use of articles, count/mass distinction in noun phrases, etc. There are other examples. It has been claimed that lack of inversion of subject and auxiliary in yes-no questions, and the use of the invariant tag "isn't it" or "no?" in tag questions are two (of the many) important features of Indian English. However, there is quite a bit of variation in the frequency of occurrence of these features, with speaker's level of education being almost certainly the major determinant. Similarly, simplification of consonant clusters (e.g., /iste:s n/ or /s te:s n/ for 'station') and insertion of glides before vowel-initial words (e.g., /yenvi/ for 'envy') have been cited as typical markers. But the strategy employed in the simplification (anaptyxis or epenthesis) depends on the speaker's mother tongue. Glide insertion is restricted to Dravidian language speakers. And, regardless of the mother tongue, whether these features occur at all and the frequency of their use depend on the speaker's education/occupational status.

The preceding discussion demonstrates the limitations of a purely linguistic (i.e., formal) analysis of a second language variety. Even more so than in the case of native varieties, second language varieties demand sociolinguistics as a congruent "level" of analysis.

Among the factors determining the occurrence of different non-native variants, the following seem to be intuitively the more important ones: (i) education and/or occupation; (ii) mother tongue; (iii) style, formal/informal; and (iv) medium, spoken/written. While some of these factors are standard in sociolinguistic theory, the mother tongue as a determinant is, of course, applicable only in the analysis of a non-native variety. It is also possible that the relative weight given to education/occupation may be different from that given in the analysis of native language variation, because the "lower" levels of the educational spectrum exhibit differences in grammar from other levels to a degree unimaginable in native varieties. The significance of medium as a determinant of variation also seems to be different in IVE contexts, where the spoken medium is marked by limited register differentiation and greater density of occurrence of non-native features. Since there has been very little systematic study of the role of these factors in non-native variation (see Platt 1975, 1977, Platt and Weber 1980 for some discussion), it is hard to be more explicit at present. I will now turn to a detailed examination of the first two of the above listed determinants.

## 3.1 Variation Based on Education/Occupation

It is widely recognized that terms such as Indian English, Nigerian English, Singapore English are abstractions. In actual fact, one encounters a continuum of language types, somewhat like the post-creole continuum described by DeCamp (1971). This range has been referred to as the cline of bilingualism (Kachru 1969), speech continuum, lectal range (Platt 1975), etc. At one end of the continuum are various types of local pidgins (used by porters, waiters, street vendors, taxi drivers, office attendants, tourist guides). Preliminary descriptions of these pidgins are found in Schuchardt (1891 [1980]), Hosali (1982), and Mehrotra (1982). These pidgins are primarily products of informal acquisition and exhibit structural features typical of pidgins described in the literature. Resulting from formal instruction in English are two types of proficiency in the language that may be called, following Platt's terminology, mesolects and acrolects. Mesolects are used by speakers with limited education (up to the first college degree) who are employed in various types of middle level occupations, for example, as school teachers, office clerks and receptionists, insurance agents, contractors, etc.). They are marked by a heavy regional accent and various types of grammatical differences from the native standard. The third type, or acrolect, is used by speakers with considerable educational qualifications who are employed as professionals, i.e., doctors, lawyers, engineers, scientists, professors, high level government officers, business executives, journalists, etc. This variety is widely understood throughout the country and abroad, and shows a wider style range though it is still noticeably distinct from the native English at every level of linguistic organization. In addition, a very small number of speakers use a variety that is not easily distinguishable from native varieties. This is generally regarded as a sign of affectation.

### 3.2 Mother Tongue Based Variation

By virtue of their use in multilingual societies, IVE's exhibit various degrees of transfer from the mother tongue. Since this type of transfer is highly patterned and regular (see Weinreich 1953, Gass and Selinker 1983), this results in recognizably distinct sub-varieties. Kachru (1976) reports that speakers of Indian English claim to be able to identify several different mother tongue-based subvarieties, such as Panjabi English, Tamil English, Bengali English, Hindi English, etc. Bamgbose (1971) has pointed out that this is true of Nigerian English as well, where Hausa, Yoruba, and Igbo speakers can be identified by their English (see also Akere 1978). The accuracy and reliability of such identifications, however, have yet to be researched.

While transfer of structural features from the mother tongue adds to the diversity of non-native varieties used in multilingual communities, it also has a unifying effect when the mother tongues in question share typological or sprachbund (areal) features. This is true of South Asia, where due to millennia of language contact, most of the languages of the area have come to share a number of formal properties (Emeneau 1956, Gumperz and Wilson 1971, Nadkarni 1975, Masica 1976) such as retroflex stops, the dative subject construction, sentential and participle relative clauses, etc. The English spoken in this area is influenced by these areal features, contributing to the structural cohesiveness of South Asian English (Kachru 1969).

### 3.3 The Notion of a Second Language Speech Community

This range of variation, baffling as it is at first glance, is perhaps not much more elaborate than that found in native varieties (cf. Cockney and Received Pronunciation in British English, and Black English and Network Standard in American English). The relevant question is whether this variation is patterned and can be explained by the familiar social and linguistic parameters. Variation per se does not negate the validity of the concept of a speech community, as is evident from the following observation by Labov,

> The speech community is not defined by any marked agreement in the use of language elements, so much as by participation in a set of shared norms; these norms may be observed in overt types of evaluative behavior, and by the uniformity of abstract patterns of variation which are invariant in respect to particular levels of usage . . . (1972:120).

There is indirect evidence that speakers of Indian English participate in a set of shared norms. For example, Willard Shaw (1981) in a survey of 825 students in Singapore, India, and Thailand, asked them to label the variety of English spoken by them. The Singaporeans were divided equally between describing their English as British English (40.5%) or a variety uniquely their own (42.3%). Half of the Indians (50.6%) indicated that a form of Indian English was prevalent, while more than a quarter (27.4%) identified British English as the norm. The Thais (speakers of a foreign language variety) were divided in their characterization of the variety they spoke: 28.1% identified with American English, 40.3% with their own variety, and 25.1% chose the option, "others". A similar pattern was found in a survey of Indian graduate students by Kachru (1976). One of the more interesting topics of research on IVE's is the acceptability of educated vs. native utterances to a range of speakers from different backgrounds.

There is also evidence of "uniformity of abstract patterns of variation" in IVE's though empirical evidence is as yet limited. Platt and Weber (1980) have shown that a number of variables (e.g., the copula in various syntactic positions, past tense marking, plural marking, consonant clusters, etc.) are sensitive to the educational/occupational status of the speakers in Singapore English. They also show that 'lect switching' is conditioned by such factors as the formality of the situation, relationship with the interlocutor, etc. In other words, IVE's seem to exhibit the same patterns of socially conditioned variation as native varieties. The second piece of evidence, as noted above, consists of the fact, noted already (cf. section 3.2), that speakers of IVE's can identify different subvarieties based on the mother tongue of the speaker. Third, IVE's themselves are sufficiently unified and distinct from one another so that speakers of other varieties are able to "place" a Nigerian or an Indian or a Filipino speaker on the basis of his or her English alone. Again, this claim is based on observation and needs to be empirically supported.

## 4. SITUATIONAL FACTORS

In this section I will examine the significance, from the viewpoint of sociolinguistic theory, of the patterns of use of IVE's. I stress that the aim is not, of course, to give a complete account of this vast topic but to draw attention to those aspects of the situation which help to explain why IVE's have the formal characteristics that they have. Let us first examine the *domains* in which English is used as a lingua franca in India. It is generally assumed that English performs this function mainly in the formal domains such as academic discussions, high level administration, law, and commerce. However, the few empirical studies available show that English is used as a contact language in other domains as well. Parasher (1980) in a survey of 350 educated bilinguals employed in several all-India level institutions and organizations in Hyderabad-Secunderabad (in South India) found that English played an important role in such informal domains as the family, friendship, neighborhood, and transactions. Although the mother tongue was far more important than English in the family domain, English was nevertheless used about 25% of the time in conversing with various members of the family. In the friendship and transactions domains it actually outranked the mother tongue by an almost two to one margin. English was the preferred choice of language in corresponding with children, siblings, and friends. In a study of 299 students and 88 employees of government and private enterprises in Bangalore, South India, the present author (see chapter 7) found that English was used extensively (though not as much as the mother tongue) in several informal domains. In certain other informal domains, English actually outpaced the mother tongue and Hindi. These findings indicate that in the urban areas at least, the role of English is not simply *complementary* with the mother tongue but is *overlapping* in certain domains. This overlap is manifested in actual usage in the form of code switching and code mixing and provides the condition for extensive mother tongue influence on the variety of English used (see chapter 4 for further discussion).

The second situational factor is *interlocutors*. The majority of speech situations in which IVE's are employed involve exchanges between speakers of the respective IVE's themselves. Interaction with native speakers of English is marginal. This observation is supported by the findings of the questionnaire survey of 825 students from Singapore, India, and Thailand by Willard Shaw referred to earlier. In response to the question "It is important for me to speak English so that I can talk to . . ." Singaporeans and Indians identified (a) "my fellow countrymen in specific social or business situations"; (b) "fellow countrymen who do not know my first language"; (c) "native English speakers"; and (d) "non-native speakers from other countries" in that order, while Thai students placed native English speakers first and their fellow countrymen last (Shaw 1981:115). This finding like all the others in Shaw's excellent study demonstrates the empirical validity of the dichotomy between indigenized and foreign language varieties. Furthermore, it shows that second language varieties are used in contexts of shared linguistic and socio-cultural norms and that their *reference groups are intra-varietal* rather than extra-varietal. This fact in turn has implications for determining the criteria of intelligibility and the instructional model in second language teaching contexts (see section 5).

The third situational factor is the *ideational content* expressed by English in indigenized variety contexts. Although English is foreign to these contexts, it is used primarily to express an indigenous socio-cultural reality. Indian English, as Kachru has emphasized in several papers (Kachru 1983a, 1986a), is used to express typically Indian socio-cultural meanings. This function is responsible not only for the occurrence of non- native lexical items but also for certain semantic and pragmatic features that have so far been less well-noticed. Take the semantic domain of kinship, for instance: Indian English uses the term *co-brother* for "wife's sister's husband" to fill a lexical gap in native English. Similarly, Nigerian English has extended the semantic range of the word *family* to include one father, several mothers, half brothers and half sisters, in addition to the concept of nuclear family usually denoted by the word (Akere 1978). In India, where vegetarianism is the norm, a meat-eater is designated by the marked term *non-vegetarian*. In the area of pragmatics, the modes of greeting, introducing, inviting, cursing, apologising, expressing hospitality and gratitude, etc., incorporate semantic formulae characteristic of the corresponding speech acts in Indian languages, which are often quite different from those of the native varieties of English (see chapter 8). These are clear cases of how the indigenous ideational content and socio-cultural norms governing verbal interactions affect the form of a second language variety.

The fourth situational factor that I wish to discuss here relates to the *role* of English within the overall verbal repertoire of the community of second language speakers. As we have already noted, in India at least, English is a predominantly urban language and is restricted (except for the pidginized varieties) to the educated segment of the population. Its use in higher education, in the influential professions, higher government functions, big time commerce, and influential news media makes it a high prestige language and a coveted asset for upward mobility (for a detailed profile of the extent of use of English in the various domains, see Sridhar 1977, 1979). The functional distribution of English relative to the mother tongue (and Hindi) is highly reminiscent of diglossic situations described by Ferguson (1959). However, the Indian situation is much more complex even in relation to the model of 'diglossia with bilingualism' discussed in Fishman (1967). While it is true that English is (a) a highly codified normative language with a respected literary tradition, (b) a formally acquired language, and (c) used in the High domains (three of the major criteria cited by Ferguson), there are several other characteristics that distinguish the contexts in which indigenized varieties are used from a typical diglossic situation. First, the codes that would be analogous to the low variety in diglossia are not really low in prestige but only relatively so in certain domains. The major languages of India such as Hindi, Telugu, Tamil, Kannada, Marathi and so on are the official languages in their respective states and have established literary traditions. In some cases they are themselves diglossic (e.g., Bengali, Tamil, Kannada, Malayalam). Second, several other codes or languages also figure in the community's repertoire. These may include, depending on the circumstances, Hindi--the official language of the federal government, the tribal or ethnic minority languages of the region (e.g., Gondi in Andhra Pradesh, Tulu in Karnataka), and classical languages (Sanskrit and Arabic). Thus the Indian situations are closer to the 'polyglossia' in Singapore described by Platt (1977) than to either Ferguson's diglossia or Fishman's diglossia with bilingualism. The multiple codes in the English speaker's repertoire participate in a complex hierarchy of relative prestige. Thus, Hindi is less prestigious than some of the regional languages (state official languages) in South India (see chapter 7), but ranks higher than the ethnic or tribal languages. Sanskrit is prestigious in the religious domain and in traditional learning. The major regional languages outrank the ethnic or tribal languages. English, however, ranks highest in prestige in all but a few domains.

This pattern of distribution of functions and their evaluation in IVE contexts explains the absence of pidgin-like characteristics such as limited vocabulary and reduction of grammatical categories--features characteristic of NNV's used in the limited or low functions.

There are two other situational factors that play a role in determining the form of English used in IVE's. These have to do with the *mode and models of acquisition.* First, English is learnt predominantly through formal instruction in second language contexts. While this does not come as a revelation, the implications of this fact have only recently come to be appreciated. It has been suggested in the literature on second language acquisition that formal learning (as opposed to informal acquisition) is more conducive to mother tongue transfer (Krashen 1978). Also, the fact that English is learnt in the overwhelming majority of cases from teachers who are themselves non-native speakers of English guarantees that the variety of English used in India will increasingly diverge from the native standards.

The discussion in this and the previous section makes it clear that both micro- and macro-sociolinguistic factors should be taken into account in explaining the formal properties of IVE's.

## 5. APPLIED SOCIOLINGUISTIC CONCERNS

Like all other non-standard varieties, second language varieties raise a number of applied sociolinguistic issues. They have to do primarily with the theory and practice of teaching English in intra- as well as international context.

Although the last two decades have been the most active period in the study of second language acquisition, there has been little attention paid to the process of acquisition of indigenized varieties. Most of the research has dealt with acquisition of a target language in contexts where it is spoken natively (e.g., English in the U.S.A. and U.K.,) and secondarily in foreign language contexts (e.g., English in Germany or Switzerland). The occasional references to the second language contexts have implied that varieties such as Indian English are fossilized stages in the acquisition of native speaker norms (Selinker 1974, see chapter 4). They also suggest that mother tongue influence is a characteristic of early stages in the acquisition process that is eventually overcome by the ideal learner (Taylor 1975, Krashen 1982). These assumptions result from an inadequate appreciation of the sociolinguistic context in which IVE's are acquired. As we have seen, the transference of patterns (lexical, pragmatic) from the mother tongue serves the important function of adapting an alien code to the socio-cultural context of use (cf. Richards 1974). Second, as several scholars have pointed out, a speaker who uses native-like pronunciation (as well as other features such as hyper-correct grammar) is viewed with suspicion and derision in second language contexts (cf. Bamgbose 1971, Eersel 1971, Tongue 1974, Tay and Gupta 1983, among others). Also, since the native models are not available to the learner and since native speakers are not the intended addressees in interactions in which these varieties are used, treating them as inadequate approximations of native norms imposes a sociolinguistically unrealistic and irrelevant standard.

Another widely held pedagogical assumption that needs to be refined in the light of data from IVE's has to do with the type of motivation considered appropriate for success in foreign language learning. In the words of Gardner and Lambert (1972),

> This theory, in brief, maintains that the successful learner of a second language must be psychologically

> prepared to adopt various aspects of behavior which characterize members of another linguistic-cultural group. The learner's ethnocentric tendencies and his attitudes toward the members of the other group are believed to determine how successful he will be, relatively, in learning the new language. His motivation to learn is thought to be determined by his attitudes toward the other group in particular and toward foreign people in general and by his orientation toward the learning task itself. The orientation is said to be *instrumental* in form if the purposes of language study reflect the more utilitarian value of linguistic achievement, such as getting ahead in one's occupation. In contrast, the orientation is *integrative* if the student wishes to learn more about the other cultural community because he is interested in it in an open-minded way, to the point of eventually being accepted as a member of that other group.

Empirical studies of language attitudes in second language contexts show that the primary motivation for learning English is "instrumental" in the sense defined above. For example, in Willard Shaw's survey referred to earlier, 95% of Singaporeans and 94% of Indians ranked "I studied English because I will need it for my work" at the top of the list of 25 possible reasons for studying English (Shaw 1981: 110). Similar results have been reported for the Philippines by Gardner and Lambert (1972) and Bombay, India by Lukmani (1972). These results have to be interpreted with reference to the common observation that countries like Singapore and India "maintain a generally high standard in the learning of English" (Shaw 1981: 112; see also Bansal 1969, Smith and Rafiqzad 1979). These studies have two important implications for sociolinguistic theory. One is that instrumental motivation *can* contribute to successful language learning. The second is that integrative motivation need not necessarily involve identification with the native speakers of the target language and a desire to be accepted as a member of that group. Lukmani has observed that her subjects viewed themselves as "based in their own country but reaching out to modern ideas and life styles" (1972:272). The reference group may well be a community of non-native users of the language being learnt. Viewed in this perspective, the integrative and instrumental motivations need not be opposed to each other. Sociolinguistics and pedagogical theory have to recognize and deal with the fact that the extended use of a language beyond its native habitat may entail the dissociation of that language from its original cultural accoutrements. This in turn should have far-reaching implications for selection of reading materials, specification of learning outcomes and the training of teachers.

The third applied topic is the choice of instructional models in second language contexts, the basic issue being the acceptability of localized forms of English (Strevens 1982) in place of the traditional native speaker standards. Since this topic has been discussed extensively in the literature (Prator 1968, Kachru 1976, 1982a, Wong 1982, among others), I will not repeat the arguments here. Suffice it to say that a strong case has been made for recognizing standard forms of national second language varieties as instructional models on the following grounds: (a) these varieties function chiefly in intra-national domains, (b) the use of native varieties is considered affected and inappropriate in second language contexts, (c) there is empirical evidence supporting the intra-regional and international intelligibility of the standard non-native varieties, (d) externally imposed models have not succeeded in the past in impeding the natural forces of language evolution, and (e) the logistics of implementing native speaker standards in second language contexts are prohibitively complex and expensive. Notwithstanding these arguments, the advisability of encouraging indigenzied varieties as instructional models has been questioned recently by no less a respected authority than Sir Randolph Quirk (1983, 1985). Quirk questions the currently 'fashionable' skepticism regarding the value of the standard of the second language among sociolinguists such as Trudgill (1975). Citing Bolinger's (1980:181) "law of communicative responsibility", he says,

> he (Bolinger) and others have also pointed out that it is perhaps disingenuous if not actually irresponsible for linguists and educationists, secure in their own acrolectal language command, to encourage the belief that other forms of language can provide the user with equal security. (1983:14-15)

He adds,

> It is at least arguable that ESL countries as different as Nigeria and Singapore need a basically monovarietal "exoglossic", international form of English as much as Germany, Japan and Russia do. (1983:14-15)

Quirk's position is predicated on the following assumptions: (1) that there is "a relatively narrow range of purposes for which the non-native needs to use English (even in ESL countries)" (1985: 6); (2) that the indigenous languages, rather than English, are the (primary) vehicle for self-expression as well as for the sustaining of traditional cultural values in second language contexts; and (3) that the arguments for not imposing the standard variety on speakers of non-standard varieties, even if they may be right for the native English speaking community, are not necessarily "exportable" to second language situations like Nigeria or Singapore.

It is instructive to examine Quirk's assumptions in some detail. His first assumption is contradicted by the overwhelming evidence for the extensive range of functions that English performs in second language contexts (see sections 2 and 3 above). His second assumption is also questionable. While it is true that the indigenous languages are the primary vehicles for the maintenance of traditional culture and values, an examination of the content of books and articles produced by users of second language varieties leaves no doubt that English plays an extremely significant role in the discussion and dissemination of indigenous social, cultural, economic, political, and even religious and philosophical issues. English is also being used increasingly as a medium of creative expression as witnessed by the vibrancy of literatures in English written in these varieties (S. N. Sridhar 1982, Thumboo 1985), and the status of English as one of the languages recognized by the Indian Literary Academy. The justification for Quirk's third assumption regarding the non-exportability of sociolinguistic theories is not clear. If the argument is that developing countries need an internationally intelligible form of English for purposes of technology transfer etc., it is not a strong one. There is empirical evidence (Bansal 1969. Smith and Rafiqzad 1979, Nelson 1982 among others) that the standard forms of indigenous varieties *are* internationally intelligible; in fact, preliminary findings suggest that certain types of standard non-native varieties may be *more* intelligible than native varieties because of their phonological characteristics such as fewer vowel reductions, elisions, etc. On the other hand, if the argument is that a global standard of English is a goal to which the development of national/regional languages should be sensitive, then it is an argument that affects the independent evolution of *languages* such as French and Japanese as much as second language *varieties* of English.

## 6. CONCLUSION

A careful study of indigenized varieties of English shows that they are qualitatively different from the categories recognized in current sociolinguistic typology. IVE's also provide some of the clearest evidence of socio-cultural determination of language variation, both on the micro- and macro- levels. An adequate account of these varieties calls for the descriptive techniques and explanatory power of the variationist, interactionist, and sociology of language paradigms within sociolinguistic theory. The circumstances of their acquisition and their viability as modes of communication argue for a reevaluation of some of the traditional assumptions about second language acquisition and teaching.

# Chapter 4

# Bridging the Paradigm Gap:
## Second Language Acquisition Theory and Indigenized Varieties of English

### 1. INTRODUCTION

Theories of Second Language Acquisition (SLA, hereafter), by and large, have been developed and tested without serious reference to data from the acquisition of English in those settings where indigenized varieties of English (IVE's, hereafter) such as Indian English, Singapore English, Nigerian English, and Filipino English play institutionalized roles.[2] On the other hand, most studies dealing with the description and acquisition of IVE's do not engage current theoretical concerns nor employ rigorous empirical methods. This chapter attempts to analyze the reasons for this absence of dialogue and to outline a functionally oriented paradigm that would give a more insightful account of the phenomena, and thereby a more satisfactory theory of SLA.

### 1.1 The Neglect of IVE's: Empirical and Theoretical Reasons

Current theoretical and empirical studies of SLA contain few references to IVE's or their acquisition (see, for example, the textbooks by Brown 1980, Dulay, Burt, and Krashen 1982, Klein 1986, or the papers in Krashen 1981, Andersen 1983, 1984, Rutherford 1985, among others). And, as we shall see below, the few references to IVE's in the theoretical literature (e.g., Selinker 1972, Nemser 1971) either derive from assumptions which can be shown to be untenable, or are still programmatic (Andersen 1983a).

This neglect of IVE's is surprising in light of a number of facts and claims about SLA theories. First, the theories purport to be applicable to SLA in general and do not place IVE's outside their purview. Second, much of SLA theorizing (and testing) has dealt with the acquisition of English. Third, learners of IVE's are, numerically as well as in terms of the range and diversity of variables they represent, one of the most significant segments of second language acquirers in the world today. These learners, constitute, to paraphrase an observation of Arthur Kleinman (1988) (with reference to the relevance of non-Western cultures to psychiatric theory), "so huge a portion of humanity, yet so silent a presence" in second language acquisition theory.

It may be argued that this exclusion is simply a function of the theorists' unfamiliarity with the contexts in which IVE's are acquired; and that in any case, a theory is best stated in the most general manner possible, and it is up to other researchers to challenge its validity by bringing up counter examples.

The arguments seems reasonable, though only to a limited extent. While the field of SLA over the last decade or so has moved rapidly and decisively to embrace empirical methods, research on the acquisition of IVE's has remained descriptive and intuitive. A few recent studies have employed rigorous empirical methods (e.g. Apte 1980, Walwadkar 1984), but such studies are exceptions rather than the rule. Most studies in the area analyze random examples from student speech (or more commonly) writing, without giving a systematic account of such crucial details as the source of the data, the elicitation procedure employed, the regularity and representativeness of the phenomenon in question, etc. Although these data can serve as valuable sources of initial hypotheses, their contribution to the dominant research questions in the field of SLA, such as the role of transfer vis-a-vis overgeneralization, remains limited. There is an urgent need for detailed studies of the acquisition of IVE's using systematic data collection procedures, rigorous analytical methods, and explicit reporting conventions.

Granted the limitations of current studies of IVE's, the fact remains that the value of the data, however systematic, is relative to the insightfulness of the hypotheses they support or refute. Herein lies another major weakness of the available studies of the acquisition of IVE's. Most of the studies in this area are derivative: they start out with an uncritical acceptance of the theoretical axioms and hypotheses presented in the "mainstream" SLA research and do little more than *illustrate* the hypothesized learner strategies, such as transfer, overgeneralization, simplification, etc. (e.g., Wong 1983) or the operation of Slobin's "charges to language" (Richards 1982), using IVE examples. To be sure, such studies may have their use, for example, as pedagogical tools in courses on SLA in countries where IVE's are used. But they contribute little to theory construction or validation because of their empirical limitations and openness to alternative analyses. What is needed is a reevaluation of the applicability of "mainstream" SLA theories to the particular circumstances in which IVE's are acquired, rather than simply legitimizing IVE learners as "normal" second language acquirers according to currently fashionable models.

The empirical limitations of the studies of the acquisition of IVE's outlined above can only be a partial explanation for the failure of SLA theory to account for IVE's. This failure stems from a number of *theory-internal* limitations as well, limitations that have prevented the field from taking a broad enough perspective. For, over the last two decades, there has developed a large body of insightful, though descriptive, literature on IVE's that has not been taken into account in proposing theories of SLA. As a result, the current theoretical paradigm of SLA has turned out to be too parochial and of limited value in explaining the distinctive characteristics of SLA in the context of IVE's. We hope that an analysis of these limitations will contribute toward a better understanding of the dynamics of the acquisition of IVE's, and hence to a more general and explanatory theory of SLA.

The descriptions of IVE's demonstrate that the settings where IVE's are acquired and used (South Asia, Southeast Asia, West and East Africa, among others) are markedly different from those presupposed in the theoretical literature on SLA (see Kachru 1982, 1983a, 1985; Smith 1981, Platt and Weber 1980, Spencer 1971, Pride 1982, Noss 1983, Llamzon 1969, Baily and Gorlach 1982, Platt, Weber and Ho 1984, Crewe 1977, Tongue 1974, Ubahakwe 1979, among others). It would be instructive to contrast these as a preliminary to a discussion of how concentration on one type of setting to the exclusion of the other may lead to the theory's loss of explanatory power.

## 2. ASSUMPTIONS UNDERLYING SLA THEORIES AND RESEARCH

SLA theories' neglect and their consequent lack of relevance to IVE's derive from a number of implicit and explicit assumptions about SLA that underlie the theories and much of the empirical work in the area. The first of these is the assumption that the *goal* of SLA is, or ought to be, to acquire native-like competence in the target language (not only in terms of pronunciation and grammatical norms but also in the range of speech acts, styles, register differentiation, and so on), and hence that the success of the learner's acquisition is to be judged accordingly. Second, it is assumed that the *input* available to the learner is extensive and intensive enough to permit acquisition of the full range of active competence in the target language. Third, the process of SLA is studied without reference to the *functions that the second language is expected to perform* for the learner and in the learner's community. Fourth, the *role of the learner's first language* is evaluated strictly with reference to its contribution in interfering with or (less frequently) facilitating the structures of the target language, and no attention is paid to its contribution to the communicative function at hand. Fifth, it is assumed that the ideal *motivation* for success in second language learning is what is called "integrative" motivation, that is, one that involves admiration for the native speakers of the language and a desire to become a member of their culture. Finally, the lion's share of *research attention* has gone to the acquisition of phonology and syntax at the expense of the study of the acquisition of the lexicon, and until recently, pragmatics.

## 3. CHARACTERISTICS OF IVE ACQUISITION SETTINGS

The acquisitional environment of IVE's differs from those which have been the focus of theorizing and experimentation in SLA in a number of ways. We will discuss a few major differences, relating to (a) the target of acquisition; (b) the input to the acquisition process; (c) the role of the acquired language in relation to the other languages in the learner's repertoire; (d) motivations of the learners; and (e) lexical and pragmatic aspects of IVE acquisition. Some of the facts stated here are quite familiar to students of IVE's, but to our knowledge, they have not been explicitly discussed in relation to the concerns of SLA theory, nor does the "mainstream" SLA literature show sufficient awareness of them.

### 3.1 The Target of Acquisition and the Interlocutors

The second language learner in target language environments (that is, in contexts where the language being learnt is the primary language of the community) is expected to be able to use the language effectively with native speakers. Hence, the intended outcome is defined in terms of the competence of the ideal native speaker of the standard variety. This assumption is extended implicitly and explicitly to second (including IVE) and foreign language contexts in pedagogic theory and practice. Virtually every book and article in the field talks about "successful" acquisition, "errors", "aberrant" or "deviant" structures, and so on, taking it as self-evident that the norm is the native standard variety.

However, the situation is different in the acquisition of an IVE. IVE's are acquired primarily for use with other speakers of IVE's (see Kachru 1976, Shaw 1981), hence, the native speaker norm is irrelevant in these contexts. In fact, as Smith (1983) has pointed out, the majority of uses of English as a second language around the world today involve interactions of one non-native speaker with another rather than the prototypical situation of a native speaker and a non-native speaker assumed in ESL textbooks. Moreover, as many studies of IVE's have pointed out (Kachru 1982a: 45, Bamgbose 1971:41, Sey 1973:1), a variety that approximates too closely the native standard (e.g., the Received Pronunciation) is "frowned upon" as "distasteful and pedantic", "affected or even snobbish." The native norm alienates the non-native speakers from their natural milieus. This is true not only of the spoken language, but apparently also of the written. Respected IVE authors speak of the need to indigenize the language to make it a suitable vehicle for carrying the weight of their Indian or African experience (Raja Rao, Chinua Achebe, to cite just two). Attitude in IVE contexts show that, although the prescriptive norms still exert their force, understandably, there is a sizeable and growing segment of teachers and learners who believe that the model of instruction should be an IVE (Kachru 1976, Shaw 1981).

## 3.2 Input

The variety of English that is available to the learners as primary input is overwhelmingly the indigenous variety of English, e.g., Indian English, West African English, etc., and not native varieties such as British or American English. In the overwhelming majority of cases, IVE's are learnt from teachers who are non-native speakers and perhaps, whose teachers were also non-native speakers. Most learners of IVE's never get to interact with a native variety speaker during their acquisition period, if ever. In fact, the spoken native varieties are hardly understandable to the learners, except in slow, deliberate speech, and even then, there are serious comprehension difficulties, which are both phonological and contextual/cultural. Second, IVE's are acquired in contexts of relatively restricted input, although not so restricted as in cases where pidgins develop. In many rural areas in Asia and Africa, for example, the learners' only exposure to English takes place in the English class at school. Although the amount of exposure to English available to the learner of an IVE is substantially more than that available in situations where English is learned as a foreign language, it is still much less than what is available to a learner of English in, say, the U.S.A., or the U.K. It is, therefore, misleading to refer to the IVE context as a *second* language context in the same sense in which the term is used for acquisition where the target language is the native language of the majority of speakers. Thirdly--a related point--the nature of the input is significantly different. The learner is not exposed to the full range of styles, structures, and speech acts that one normally associates with the use of a language as the primary vehicle of verbal communication in a society. Thus, the ordinary (non-Westernized) learner of English in India doesn't get exposed to the use of English to maintain and transact informal, everyday, affective interpersonal relationships (the mother tongue is used for these), instead, he or she gets exposed to the academic and bureaucratic registers and literary styles. The English that is heard outside of class is of little relevance to his or her interests in the early years of acquisition of English. At this stage, the learner's "intake" is effectively restricted to whatever is available in the classroom.

### 3.3 Role of IVE's in the Verbal Repertoire

Learners of IVE's go on to use English alongside other languages in their repertoire. As sociolinguistic surveys of the use of English by learners and professionals have shown (Parasher 1980, chapter 7), English functions like the H(igh) variety in a diglossic situation with respect to the other languages in a number of domains in bi- and multilingual communities. This complementarity of functions means that English is not called upon to serve *all* the functions that it may serve a monolingual English speaker, and hence, it is wrong to assume that the IVE learner should exhibit the same range of competence as the learner in a "melting pot" target language environment (See chapter 7). The model of bilingualism appropriate to the IVE contexts is, therefore, a "complementary" one and not a "replacive," or "duplicative" model.

In fact, there is empirical evidence to show that the functions of English not only complement but overlap those of the local languages in a number of domains such as friendship, correspondence, transactions, etc., (Parasher 1980, chapter 7). Code switching and code mixing are formal manifestations of this overlap. Furthermore, there is a good deal of evidence, as pointed out by Kachru (1986), that the user of English in these varieties presupposes a bilingual competence on the part of the receiver. The fact that IVE's are acquired in such contexts of intensive and extensive bilingualism is of central importance in developing explanatory models of their acquisition and use.

### 3.4 Motivation

Sociolinguistic surveys of the attitudes and motivations of IVE learners (Kachru 1976, Shaw 1981) have shown that in these settings, "the reasons for studying English and the skills desired are overwhelmingly the ones normally labelled instrumental" (Shaw 1981: 121). The effectiveness of instrumental motivation in promoting second language proficiency has been demonstrated by Lukmani (1972) for a group of "non-Westernized" women in Bombay, and by Gardner and Lambert (1972) for Filipino learners of English. As Shaw correctly points out,

> The generally high level of English ability observed [in the IVE settings] seems to throw doubt on the hypothesis that integrative motivation is essential for achievement in second [language] acquisition. At least the whole aspect of integrative motivation should be re-examined in terms of a desire among learners to join an indigenous group of English language speakers or a vague international one rather than a group of foreign native speakers (Shaw 1981:121).

### 3.5 Lexical and Pragmatic Aspects

Some of the most distinctive characteristics of IVE's involve innovations in the lexicon, collocational possibilities, and the ways in which speech acts, such as thanking, complimenting, urging, consoling, and so on are carried out in the adapted language. Unfortunately, it is precisely these areas, which reflect the distinctive cultural experiences and conventions of the community, that SLA has had little to say about, until recently (see Wolfson and Judd 1983). It is, therefore, not surprising that researchers in IVE's feel that SLA theories have failed them in that they provide no apparatus for characterizing the distinctiveness of, say, Nigerian English, even when the grammar may not deviate from the native standard.

## 4. DANGERS OF AN UNCRITICAL APPLICATION OF THE CURRENT SLA PARADIGM

The contrast between the assumptions of the current SLA paradigm and the features of IVE settings outlined above suggests that the concepts of the former are not readily transferable to the IVE situations. We shall demonstrate this point with reference to some of the more important concepts in SLA theory, such as *interlanguage*, *pidginization*, *creolization*, and most importantly, *transfer*.

The term "interlanguage" (and others used interchangeably with it, such as "approximative systems") has been used in the SLA literature to refer to a variety of "intermediate" systems between the native language and the "target language", such as the intermediate stages in the second language learners' language, immigrant varieties, institutionalized (indigenized) non-native varieties (IVE's), and different types of pidgins. For Selinker, who introduced the term in recent SLA theory, "successful" second language learners are those "who seem to achieve native speaker 'competence', i.e., those who learn a second language so that their 'performance' is indistinguishable from that of native speakers" (1974:49). According to him, "perhaps a mere 5% of all learners" achieve this competence, the rest--the overwhelming majority--end up with an interlanguage. This interlanguage is a product of a number of major processes, such as language transfer, transfer of training, second language learning strategy, second language communication strategy, overgeneralization of target language structures, and other minor ones, such as hypercorrection, spelling pronunciation, etc. The most crucial problem in SLA theory, according to Selinker, is accounting for the phenomenon of *fossilization*, i.e., "regular reappearance or re-emergence in Interlanguage productive performance of linguistic structures which were thought to be eradicated" (1974:36). Fossilizable phenomena are "linguistic items, rules, and subsystems which speakers of a particular [native language] will tend to keep in their [interlanguage] relative to a particular [target language]" (p. 36). He goes on to note that "many of these phenomena reappear in interlanguage performance when the learner's attention is focused upon new and difficult intellectual subject matter or when he is in a state of anxiety or other excitement, and strangely enough, sometimes when he is in a state of extreme relaxation" (ibid). As an example, he cites "Indian English as an Interlanguage with respect to English" which "seems to fossilize the *that* complement or *V that* construction for all verbs that take sentential complements" (p. 37). Later in the paper, he emphasizes that "not only can entire competencies be fossilized in individual learners performing in their own interlingual situation [footnote omitted], but also in whole groups of individuals, resulting in the emergence of a new dialect (here Indian English), where fossilized competencies may be the normal situation" (p. 38).

There are many problems with this account. First, although Selinker doesn't make this explicit, interlanguage as a phenomenon of SLA is an *unstable* system. Corder (1967), Nemser (1971) and many other researchers have talked about the "atypical rapidity" with which interlanguages change in the learner. The "fossilized" structures of Indian English that Selinker discusses, on the other hand, are *stable* characteristics of the variety and not only of the learners' languages, and have persisted across generations (see, for example, the accounts of Indian English in Schuchardt [1891] 1980, Whitworth 1907). Second, in Selinker's system, fossilized structures "reappear" under a special set of circumstances, e.g., conditions of anxiety, "extreme relaxation", etc. This implies that in other circumstances, non-fossilized, presumably target-like, features may be used. Again, this is not representative of the majority of IVE users. For the majority of speakers of Indian English, the so-called "fossilized" structures are the "normal" structures and they have none others in their competence. Third, the application of the term interlanguage to IVE's suggests that they represent an intermediate *acquisitional stage* on their way toward a native or native-like norm. As we have seen, the *acquisitional target* for IVE speakers is not the native norm but an indigenized one.

Calling the IVE's interlanguages or their structural features fossilizations does violence to both the phenomena in question and to the theoretical constructs.

Equally unilluminating are some of the other concepts used in current SLA theory, such as "pidginization" and "creolization" (for a discussion of how IVE's do not fit into the current sociolinguistic typologies, see chapter 3). Despite Andersen's (1983b) admirable attempt to untangle the issues in this area (cf. Andersen 1983a), one cannot help agreeing with Sankoff's observation that "we have about reached the limits of the potential usefulness of the terms "pidginization" and "creolization" (Sankoff 1983:242). For, pidginization in process terms has come to be a shorthand expression for "component processes" of second language acquisition such as "simplification", "negative transfer", and so on--which are themselves agonizingly difficult to distinguish from one another--which seem to obtain in *all* non-primary language acquisition. The term is also plainly misleading in that it suggests that the outcome would be a pidgin while it is not. In any case, the concept is inappropriate for IVE's for at least two reasons: a) as noted above, the restricted input that the IVE learner has access to is not so restricted as to prevent him/her from becoming a bilingual in it; b) the structural modifications involved in the learning and evolution of IVE's include at least as much *complexification* as simplification.

The concept of "creolization" as a model of IVE acquisition appears at first sight to be more appropriate than pidginization, for it seems to capture several important characteristics of IVE's. These include, to use a slightly modified version of Andersen's (1983a:31-32) typology: the use of English forms with non-English meaning, function, and distribution; non-English meanings, forms, and distributions (at least partially) derived from the substrate languages; non-English structures (at least partially) determined by Slobin's cognitive and perceptual constraints, such as his famous "operating principles" and "charges to language" (see Slobin 1973 and 1982), as well as from linguistic universals; innovations already present in the input. However, this is creolization only metaphorically; for, as Bickerton (1983:238) observes, creolization is done mainly by children; the learners have an "abnormal" language background; it gives you a first language, not a second. Once again, it is clear that there is no substitute to studying the phenomena empirically, sui generis, and postponing pigeonholing until we have a clearer understanding of what actually goes on in the acquisition of IVE's.

While the attempts to fit IVE's into the current theoretical constructs of SLA have been unsuccessful and misleading, the neglect of IVE's has also been detrimental to the development of SLA theory. As an example of this, we shall discuss the treatment of the role of transfer in the acquisition process. The contrastive analysis hypothesis has had an interesting and complicated history in second language acquisition (see S. N. Sridhar 1980 for a historical overview and Gass and Selinker 1983 for some recent studies), so our discussion will be limited to its relevance to the understanding of indigenized varieties.

SLA theory in the 1970's dismissed the role of the mother tongue in acquisition as marginal, if not irrelevant, especially in syntax, thanks to the misleading correlation between transfer and behaviorist learning theory proposed first in Dulay and Burt (1974) and repeated in Dulay, Burt, and Krashen (1982). The negative evaluation of transfer in pedagogical circles, and the preoccupation of the overwhelming majority of empirical studies of SLA with acquisition in native variety settings also contributed to the downplaying of transfer. In this climate of opinion, it became fashionable to reinterpret putative cases of transfer as outcomes of such other 'respectable' acquisition strategies as overgeneralization (e.g., Jain 1974). As Y. Kachru (1980) has shown, many alleged instances of overgeneralization can equally plausibly be shown to be consistent with a theory of transfer. Of late, even apparently 'clear' cases of transfer (such as the retention of resumptive pronouns in relative clauses by Arab and Persian learners) have come to be interpreted as due to the learners' selection of unmarked parameter settings (Hyltenstam 1984).

However, anyone familiar with the formal and pragmatic characteristics of IVE's can not fail to be struck by the fact that many of these features can be related to features of the speakers' mother tongue in a fairly transparent fashion (cf. Kachru (1983a), Bokamba (1982), Platt and Weber (1980), and chapter 8, among others). And, given that transfer, as a process, is perfectly consistent with a 'cognitivist' (i.e., hypothesis formation and testing) theory of second language acquisition (see chapter 5 and also S. N. Sridhar 1980), there seems to be little motivation for being apologetic about claiming IVE's to be, in good part, products of transfer. Indeed, Quirk et al. (1972) refer to IVE's as 'interference varieties'. We prefer the term 'transfer' to 'interference' because of the apparent negative connotations of the latter. This is, of course, not to deny that there are other processes operating to produce the structural and pragmatic characteristics of IVE's.

In fact, recent research (e.g., the papers in Gass and Selinker 1983) shows that what is at issue is not the operation of transfer as a significant process in second language acquisition, but the conditions under which transfer operates. In this connection, it is interesting to note Ervin-Tripp's observation that (more) mother tongue influence is found in "learning conditions in which the second language was not the language of the learner's larger milieu so that the learning contexts were aberrant both in function and frequency of structures" (1974:121). This observation, though based on foreign language learning contexts, is applicable, mutatis mutandis, to IVE's as well, though Ervin-Tripp's characterization of the contexts of limited exposure as "aberrant" is disturbing. This is an example of how the preoccupation with acquisition in target language environments had led to a loss of perspective. SLA researchers seem to overlook the fact, which scholars of IVE have been stressing for quite some time (Kachru 1976, Strevens 1982), that many times more learners acquire second languages in contexts of limited exposure than in target or host language environments. Muysken (1984) seems to be one of the few researchers in SLA to take note of this fact. He observes, "L2 learning modeled on the speech productions of L2 speakers may well be the norm, worldwide, rather than the exception" (p. 102).

Crucial to the understanding of the role of transfer in IVE's is a recognition of the roles of the language being acquired (and used) in the learner's verbal repertoire. As we have seen above (see also chapter 1), English in multilingual contexts such as in India or Singapore complements and overlaps with the other languages in the bilingual's repertoire and it is used to interact with other bilinguals. As a result, the user of English expects bilingual competence in his or her interlocutors. Because of this shared bilingual repertoire, transfer of elements from the shared languages is not an obstacle to easy communication. Far from impeding intelligibility, transfer acts as the grease that makes the wheels of bilingual communication turn smoothly. Given that transfer features are not idiosyncratic to learners but shared by speakers with the same substratal languages, they serve as effective simplification strategies, modes of acculturation (see Lowenberg 1986) and as markers of membership in the community of speakers of a given indigenized variety (see Gumperz 1964) for a similar analysis of Panjabi-Hindi bilingualism in India). In cases of pragmatic transfer, for example, where the semantic formulae characteristic of a speech act in the mother tongue are transferred in the performance of analogous speech acts in English, even though the native variety might employ a different set of semantic formulae (see Olshtain and Cohen, 1983 and also chapter 8), transfer serves as an effective strategy of acculturation which draws upon shared cultural presuppositions. Thus, transfer in an indigenized variety does not have the same negative value--in terms of either potential interference with intelligibility or attitudinal devaluation--that it seems to have in the acquisition of a native variety in a monolingual target language setting. In other words, the functions of transfer in second language contexts are not in principle different from those in language contact situations in general. In studies of language contact, it is expected and accepted that borrowed items undergo change due to acculturation and linguistic assimilation (see, for example, Weinreich 1953, Haugen 1972). Similarly, given that all the languages of the learner's repertoire are actively used in second language contexts, it is to be expected that the languages interact with one another's formal features.

The abhorrence of transfer derives from an artificial view of bilingual language storage and processing based on two questionable assumptions: one is that the ideal bilingual keeps his or her languages separate--both in storage and in actual use (a view that derives from Weinreich 1953); the other assumption is that the ideal bilingual is as proficient in each of his or her languages as the ideal native speaker of the respective languages (cf. Bloomfield 1933). There is ample evidence that both of these assumptions are wrong. As we shall see in Chapter 6, linguistic and psycholinguistic evidence argues for an interactional model of bilingual processing as opposed to the so-called 'separate storage' hypothesis. Grosjean (1982) has persuasively argued for a notion of bilingual competence in which the languages in the repertoire complement one another's strengths and weaknesses to produce the type of composite language competence suited to the demands on the bilingual. In addition, linguistic and sociolinguistic studies of code mixing in communities where IVE's are used have shown that English and the local languages operate in complex syntactic relationships within single sentences (Annamalai 1971, Kachru 1978, S. N. Sridhar 1978, Poplack 1978, Pfaff 1979, among others). Given that such mixing is the *norm* for the type of language situation that the learner is exposed to and hence the type of language that he or she will be called upon to use, it is hardly surprising that transfer should play a *central* part in the acquisition process. It is unrealistic prescriptivism to evaluate the success of second language learning with reference to transfer-free norms in such contexts.

The dangers of ignoring the bilingual's repertoire in SLA are also illustrated by Dan Egbe's (1979) discussion of the acquisition of English by Nigerian learners. Observing that Nigerian learners tend to use formal polite terms where informal polite expressions would be appropriate in native varieties, Egbe argues that this is not a deficiency in their English but a consequence of the availability of Nigerian Pidgin English for informal uses. Similar arguments can be offered for the alleged 'gaps' in the learners' competence noted in other indigenized varieties. In devising measures of acquisitional success or accuracy, it is therefore necessary to take into account the functions that the learner's language is intended to serve, rather than assume that the learner aims at acquiring the full range of native competence in English.

There are many other areas of SLA theory where putatively universal concepts and processes have been proposed without taking note of potential contradiction from IVE data. A case in point is Kellerman's (1978) claim that items that appear to be language-specific (e.g., idioms) will be less prone to transfer. No one familiar with the literature on Indian or West African English, let alone the literature *in* those IVE's (see S. N. Sridhar 1982) could even entertain such a claim. The fact that such ridiculous propositions remain unchallenged for years is a sad commentary on the narrow theoretical and empirical foundations of current SLA theories.

Yet, there are some signs that this situation might be changing. Andersen (1983b:17) lists "indigenized language" as a distinct "setting or type of acquisition" in his typology of second language acquisition contexts and processes and, classifies IVE's as "creoloids" (following Platt 1977), rather than creoles. Muysken (1984)--working independently of IVE's--advocates a perspective on SLA that corresponds to the paradigm argued for in this paper and in the literature on IVE's (see, e.g., Kachru 1983, 1986):

> to see second language learning as becoming a member of a speech community, governed in the same way as other forms of verbal behavior by the norms that obtain in that particular speech community (p. 101).

Welcome aboard!

## 5. CONCLUSION

The foregoing discussion demonstrates that there is a lack of articulation between theories of second language acquisition and research on the acquisition and use of indigenized varieties of English. On the one hand, the theories have either overextended the constructs based on acquisition in monolingual, target language settings, giving a distorted picture of IVE's, or ignored them altogether. Thus, SLA theory has been counter-intuitive and limited in explanatory power with regard to a very substantial segment of the second language learner population. Studies of IVE's, on the other hand, have remained descriptive and atheoretical, rather than based on rigorous and systematic empirical research. Thus, the IVE's distinctiveness from the prototypes assumed in SLA theories has not been convincingly demonstrated. This paper has been a modest attempt to show that, despite the absence of empirical research on the acquisition of IVE's, attention to the particular situations in which they are acquired and used, and especially their roles in the communicative patterns of their multilingual societies, will contribute to a broadening of perspective and re-evaluation of the universal applicability of many of the concepts employed in current SLA theory. Paradoxical as it may seem, second language acquisition researchers seem to have neglected the fact that the goal of second language acquisition is bilingualism. Attention to indigenized varieties of English may help remind us of this useful idea and contribute to the formulation of a more widely applicable--if more complex--theory of second language acquisition.

# Chapter 5

# Cognitive Educational Psychology and Second Language Acquisition Strategies

## 1. INTRODUCTION

Recent advances in linguistic theory and empirical studies of first and second language acquisition have been interpreted as calling for a cognitive (as opposed to a behaviorist) model of language learning. With few exceptions, the dominant model of language teaching in schools and colleges has, however, been based on a behavioristic model. This is not because a cognitivist model of the psychology of learning is not available: the models of David Ausubel and Robert Gagne--to name only the two most influential theorists--are quite well known in the field of education. The problem seems to be that the task of first or second language acquisition, especially the latter, has not been analyzed in light of this framework, with the exception of some global analogies by Brown (1980) and Seliger (to appear). In this paper I would like to relate what is known about second language acquisition to the principles of learning outlined in the cognitivist model of David Ausubel. I will also point out some important pedagogical implications that follow from this relationship.

## 2. A MODEL OF LANGUAGE COMPETENCE

As Chomsky (1959) pointed out in his epoch-making review of Skinner's *Verbal Behavior* (1957), a crucial criterion for the adequacy of any learning theory is that it should take into account the properties of the cognitive domain whose learning is explained by the theory. In other words, a theory of the learning of chess must at least take note of the properties of the game of chess, for example, the way in which chess differs from football. Chomsky criticized Skinner for ignoring the unique properties of language as a cognitive domain, and for assuming that the process of learning is the same, regardless of what is learned. Ausubel and Gagne also make the same point and blame this simplistic assumption for "much of the current confusion regarding the nature of learning" (Ausubel et al., 1978:32). In order to avoid falling into the same trap, let us briefly recall the kind of skills that constitute linguistic competence before we consider the adequacy of a cognitive learning theory for this domain. Needless to say, what follows is neither an exhaustive nor a detailed account of what constitutes linguistic competence: it is a selective, simplified, illustrative sketch of the types of skills that are involved.

### 2.1 Types of Linguistic Skill

The language learner must be able to demonstrate through his or her productive and receptive behavior a knowledge of (1) which distinctions of sound are phonemic and which are allophonic; (2) what combinations of sounds can and do occur in actual or potential words of the language; (3) what sounds can occur in what positions; (4) how sounds change as a result of the environments in which they occur; (5) patterns of stress and intonation at the word, constituent, and sentence levels and how these relate to the grammatical, semantic, and pragmatic levels; (6) the relationships between sound or letter sequences and meanings, i.e., words; (7) the grammatical classes to which words belong, how words are modified and derived by the presence of grammatical morphemes, and the constraints on these processes; (8) how words relate to one another in terms of synonymy, antonym, homophony, entailment, contradiction, redundancy, etc.; (9) how words group with other words to form constituents of various types and the constraints on the internal structure of constituents, for example, in terms of word order, co-occurrence, etc.; (10) rules specifying the possible combination of constituents i.e., optional versus obligatory presence or absence of elements that define the notion of a possible sentence; (11) rules of co-occurrence of elements and modification of a given element due to the presence of some other element; (12) the systematic structural and semantic relationships between sentences, for example, via transformations; (13) the meanings of sentences resulting from their syntactic structure as opposed to the sum of the meanings of their parts; (14) the pragmatic and sociolinguistic conditions on the appropriate use of lexical items as well as sentence types, and so on and so forth. (See, Smith and Wilson 1979 for an insightful discussion of this topic).

## 3. AUSUBEL'S COGNITIVE THEORY OF LEARNING

Ausubel makes a distinction between various types of learning. A basic distinction is between Reception Learning and Discovery Learning, each of which is further subdivided into Rote or Meaningful Learning. In Reception Learning, "the entire content of what is to be learned is presented to the learner in final form. The learning task does not involve any independent discovery on the learner's part" (p. 42). The learning of arbitrary sound-meaning correspondences in words can be viewed as an example of Reception Learning. In Discovery Learning, on the other hand, "the principal content of what is to be learned is not given but must be discovered by the learner before it can be meaningfully incorporated into the students' cognitive structure" (p. 24). One example of discovery is the insight that the final *-ed* ending on verbs indicates past tense in English. This process may involve, as a prerequisite, rearrangement of input material into a pattern which facilitates perception of the "common attributes of a number of diverse instances" (ibid).

Ausubel also makes an orthogonal distinction between Meaningful versus Rote learning. He emphasizes that "both reception and discovery learning can be either rote or meaningful depending on the conditions under which learning occurs" (p. 27). Rote learning, according to Ausubel, occurs "if the learning task consists of purely arbitrary associations . . . (as in Serial Learning), if the learner lacks the relevant prior knowledge necessary for making the learning task potentially meaningful, etc. (p. 27). Meaningful learning occurs "if the learning task can be related in non-arbitrary, substantive (not verbatim) fashion to what the learner already knows" (p. 27). The learning of the sound-letter correspondences in reading and writing as well as perhaps the gender of nouns in languages such as German and Hindi are examples of Rote learning. The learning of foreign language words as equivalents of words or ideas in the learner's mother tongue is an example of Meaningful learning because there is a non-arbitrary relationship, namely that of semantic equivalence between the new word and the word or idea already present in the learner's cognitive structure. In addition to non-arbitrariness, the other criterion of Meaningful learning is "substantive relatability", i.e., the new material is ideationally equivalent to elements existing within the learner's cognitive structure. In other words, the new concept or term may be translated without change of meaning into a concept or a set of concepts already present in the learner's cognitive structure. For example, a zebra is substantially relatable to the proposition: a horse with black and white stripes.

### 3.1 Assimilation

The centerpiece of Ausubel's cognitive theory of learning is the notion of assimilation. "The interactive role that existing cognitive structures play" (p. v) is so important that the theory itself is labelled assimilation theory. Ausubel emphasizes that the core of the assimilation process is the interaction between the new and existing knowledge. The new material is itself modified by the existing knowledge in the process of assimilation just as much as the pre-existing cognitive structure is reorganized by the new knowledge. To give a crude analogy, we see in the world only what our eyeglasses allow us to see and our conception of the world changes constantly with the assimilation of new knowledge. This interactionist character of assimilation theory sets it apart from the stimulus-response or associationist theories.

Before I go on to elaborate the different ways in which the old and the new knowledge interact, let me give an example of such interaction from language learning so as to keep the discussion concrete and relevant. The example comes from the acquisition of distinctive features in child language learning. Neil Smith in his well-known book *The Acquisition of Phonology* (1973) observes that a child may at one stage fail to distinguish between voiced and voiceless sounds, thus producing, for example, 'pig' and 'big' in the same manner. But at a later stage, once the voicing distinction is learned, he or she applies it across the board to all the relevant words in his or her vocabulary, thus distinguishing not only 'pig' and 'big', but also 'fine' and 'vine', and so on. One could argue that what happens in such cases is that the discovery of the voicing contrast results in a restructuring or reinterpretation of the pre-existing cognitive structure.

Ausubel postulates several internal cognitive processes involved in assimilation. The most important of these are : (1) Subsumption (i.e., Subordinate Learning); (2) Superordinate learning; (3) Combinatorial Learning.

#### 3.1.1 *Subsumption*

Subsumption takes place when new information is linked to an already existing idea. This linkage can be of one or two types: the new idea may be linked as a further example of the existing concept, for instance, when the language learner learns the word 'eat' is a verb. Note that the concept of the verb is not changed, only a new example is added. This type of subordinate learning is called Derivative Subsumption.

A second type of linkage obtains when a piece of new information results in an extension, modification, or qualification of an existing concept. An example is when a learner discovers that complements of verbs can not only be tensed clauses as in "Mary believes that she is honest," but also infinitive and possessive-'ing gerundive clauses, e.g., "Mary believes him to be honest," and "Mary opposes John's promoting Gertrude." Notice that here the new learning brings about a change in the existing concept of a verbal complement. This type of linkage is called Correlative Subsumption.

### 3.1.2 *Superordinate Learning*

Superordinate Learning is a second major type of learning where the existing ideas are seen as instantiations of a new superordinate concept. An example might be the discovery that words like 'can', 'may', 'shall', 'will', etc., all are examples of the class 'auxiliary', which is defined by a new set of critical properties or attributes (e.g., in terms of position in the verb phrase, movement in question formation, lack of stress, co-occurrence with contracted negatives, ability to inflect for tense, etc.).

### 3.1.3 *Combinatorial Learning*

Combinatorial Learning is the third internal cognitive process, where a new idea is seen to be related to existing ideas but not in a superordinate or subordinate relationship. An example might be the notion of the subject as a grammatical category, or number and gender as verbal categories that are not necessarily subsumed under a more abstract notion of grammatical category as such.

## 4. APPLICABILITY TO LANGUAGE LEARNING

Viewing Ausubel's theory in light of the sample inventory of language skills presented earlier, it becomes apparent that this cognitive theory is particularly suited to the domain of language learning. First of all, there is an explicit recognition of the systematicity of the learner's knowledge of the language at any given point of time. This recognition follows from the assumption that knowledge always exists in an organized fashion in the cognitive structure. This gives a natural explanation for the internally consistent nature of language output by the learner at a given stage (cf. Corder 1967) and also accounts for the across the board application of new learning leading to the next stage. For example, it is often noted that in learning to form questions, the learner goes through a stage in which all of his questions lack subject-auxiliary inversion, whereas in the next stage the appropriate change in word order is found in all applicable cases. Secondly, the learning of vocabulary has long been recognized as involving both superordinate and subordinate learning.

Third, in the learning of syntax, the notion of anchorage of new ideas to existing cognitive structure becomes especially relevant. The syntax of any language is marked by extremely rich patterns of inter-relationship. Certain types of syntactic rules or processes figure repeatedly in various parts of the language. Consider for example, subject-auxiliary inversion in English. This is used both in "yes-no questions" and "wh-questions". Consider again the movement of a *wh*-word to the beginning of a clause. This is found both in relative clauses and *wh*-questions. Or the dependency relation between a pronoun and its antecedent, in the example, "John told me that he is sick", is found both in pronominalization and reflexivization. If the learner already knows any of these processes, in either structure, it would serve as an anchor for the learning of these processes in the other structures.

Another extremely powerful anchor would be the regularity in the behavior of syntactic constituents. Once the learner grasps the notion of say, the noun phrase as a constituent, he will find it easy to understand why such a constituent can function as subject, direct object, object of preposition, etc., of sentences. In other words, previously *arbitrary* information about what sorts of elements can occur as subject, object, etc., becomes *meaningful* with the introduction of the notion of a constituent. This is an example of superordinate learning that goes a long way in language acquisition. The theory of assimilation also provides a beautiful way of teaching and learning how transformations operate in terms of constituents. One cannot go very far in syntax without the notion of the constituent as a cognitive unit with its own internal structure and semantic coherence.

## 5. IMPLICATIONS FOR SECOND LANGUAGE TEACHING

One can go on listing aspects of language structure that are explainable in terms of the cognitive learning theory. However, let me turn now to a different question, namely, the implications of Ausubel's theory for second language teaching. Ausubel himself discusses this in very broad outline in his book: specifically his observations are phrased in terms of an opposition to the audio-lingual method. He notes correctly that the emphasis on mechanical drills encourages rote learning as opposed to meaningful learning. While this may be suitable for learning items which are related to one another in an arbitrary fashion, this technique is unsuitable when the learning material exhibits non-arbitrary, systematic, and predictable internal structure. What is more, since the object of language learning is to acquire a creative command of the language rather than a finite list of sentences, the pattern drill technique is not theoretically consistent with its aims.

The second implication is of a more radical nature, and is based on a recognition of the difference between the child and adult learner in cognitive equipment. While the child has no choice but to learn language inductively, i.e., through discovery learning, there is no reason why this procedure should be followed in second language learning. The adult learner has the cognitive maturity to handle abstract propositions and categories such as noun, verb, sentence, subject, agreement, etc. By making use of the learner's cognitive structure, it should be possible to avoid laborious inductive discovery and, instead, achieve the same results more efficiently in a shorter time by using a partly deductive approach. It may be noted that this also goes against the dictum of some of the stronger versions of the audio-lingual method, namely, to avoid grammatical explanations. However, the rationale for avoiding explanations has never been convincingly presented. What one finds is a confusion between using explanations and being prescriptive. In some cases, it is argued that explanation would only confuse or be incomprehensible. If the explanation is specific, clear, unambiguous, and relatable to the concepts already known to the learner, it becomes both comprehensible and useful. These are indeed characteristics of introductory and summatory material that Ausubel calls "organizers".

In light of current research on second language acquisition and theories about the role of the learner's first language, perhaps the most significant and controversial implication of Ausubel's theory is the central place of "transfer" in the learning process. The existence of transfer is, of course, entirely consistent with the assumptions of the theory. If the meaningful learning involves an interaction between known and new information, it follows that the nature of existing knowledge should play a major role in determining what is learned and how. Indeed, Ausubel et al go so far as to claim that "If we had to reduce all of Educational Psychology to just one principle we would say this, the most important single factor influencing learning is what the learner already knows. Ascertain this and teach him accordingly" (p. 163).

In the case of the second language learner, the most important element of what he or she already knows is, of course, his native language. Therefore, Ausubel claims explicitly that "transfer" from the mother tongue is the single most important cognitive structure variable in second language learning. Consequently, Contrastive Analysis, which aims to "ascertain what he already knows" would play a central part in the teaching method based on this theory. In view of the recent controversy about both the role of interference as a learning strategy and the predictive adequacy of Contrastive Analysis, it is instructive to examine Ausubel's claim in detail.

## 5.1 Transfer in Cognitive Theory

First of all, it may be noted that there is a tendency in the empirical studies of second language acquisition to downplay the role of native language interference in favor of explaining errors in terms of other strategies such as overgeneralization and simplification (e.g., Dulay and Burt 1974, Felix 1978).

This rejection of interference or transfer is allegedly based on both theoretical and empirical grounds. Theoretically, it is claimed that interference is a corollary of a behavioristic learning theory, based on conditioning (Dulay and Burt, 1974). It is easy to demonstrate that this is a mistaken assumption. The notion of transfer is perfectly consistent with a mentalistic theory of learning such as that of Ausubel. Meaningful learning is a process of assimilating new information into existing cognitive structures, and modifying existing cognitive structures to accommodate new information. It follows that the existing patterns of knowledge play a crucial role in determining how new information is learned. This process of assimilation is far from a mechanical intrusion of old habits into new situations. It is an active, integrative, rule-governed process and is no more dependent on behavioristic conditioning than the child's overgeneralizations. This brings me to my next point, which is the alleged distinction between transfer and other strategies. It is claimed that there is no empirical evidence for transfer and that all purported instances of transfer are explainable in terms of other strategies such as overgeneralization. However, the evidence is far from clear. As Y. Kachru (1980) and others have pointed out, many instances of what are called overgeneralization can be explained in terms of mother-tongue patterns. In many cases, the assignment of errors to one or the other process seems to be arbitrary.

A second objection is that students from diverse language backgrounds make the same kind of error, and therefore it cannot be attributed to their mother tongue. Here again the reasoning is not quite convincing, as Schachter and Celce-Murcia (1977) have pointed out. This approach looks at only one side of the coin, namely the fact that a group of learners with mixed language backgrounds all make the same kind of error. It ignores the possibility that learners from a different language background may not make that error. It is possible that the languages whose speakers make the same kind of error share some typological characteristics which account for the shared error despite superficially different structures.

A third objection to interference is based on the alleged unreliability of the predictions of Constrastive Analysis. In many cases, this objection is based on rather crude predictions. What is often lost sight of is the fact that different types of correspondences between languages might result in different types of interference. For example, the absence of a category in the mother tongue compared to its presence in the target language may not be as serious a cause of interference as partial similarity. Even those critiques of Contrastive Analysis which take into account such differences in correspondence, for example Brown (1980), ignore the fact that there is no theoretical basis for the Hierarchy of Difficulties proposed by Stockwell et al (1965). This Hierarchy is simply an impressionistic model rather than one based on a sophisticated theory of transfer.

The foregoing discussion of the treatment of transfer in the literature on second language acquisition is intended not so much as a reactionary last ditch defense of Contrastive Analysis. My purpose has been simply to point out: (a) that the case against transfer is not as conclusive as it is sometimes made out to be; and (b) that the notion of transfer is consistent with a cognitive theory of second language acquisition.

As a matter of fact, the case for "transfer" as a cognitive structure variable goes beyond just native language interference. As several authors such as Corder (1967), S. N. Sridhar (1980) and others have pointed out, intralanguage errors such as overgeneralization, simplification, ignorance of rule restrictions, etc., involve a cognitive process similar to first language interference. In all these cases, an available hypothesis is applied to a new situation. In the case of "interference", the source of the hypothesis is the tried and tested one from the mother tongue. In other cases, the source is from within the target language. In either case, the process is one of assimilation.

## 6. CONCLUSION

Ausubel's theory of "assimi'ation", which includes various types of learning, is particularly suited to account for the learning of an internally structured complex domain, such as language. I have attempted, in this chapter, to analyze a few aspects of language learning as examples of the types of cognitive processes outlined by Ausubel. A more detailed analysis of various types of linguistic skills would point out, it seems to me, not only the richness of the cognitive theory in question but also possibly the need to elaborate and extend the theory to account for more complex linguistic phenomena than I have included here. Once this is done, the next step would be to relate the specific cognitive processes involved in learning different types of linguistic skills with cognitively based teaching strategies appropriate to those skills.

# Chapter 6

# The Syntax and Psycholinguistics of Bilingual Code Mixing

## 1. INTRODUCTION

Uriel Weinreich's characterization of the ideal bilingual as an individual 'who switches from one language to the other according to appropriate changes in speech situation (interlocutors, topic, etc.), *but not in an unchanged speech situation, and certainly not within a single sentence*' (1963:73, emphasis added) seems to have had an enormous impact on the direction of research in linguistics and, especially, in psychology over the last two decades. While linguists have concentrated on the situational determinants of code switching, psychologists have focused on the bilingual's remarkable ability to keep his language systems separate. In the process, the phenomenon of switching between languages 'in an unchanged speech situation' and 'within a single sentence' has been neglected. It was often considered either a sign of incomplete learning or a pathological condition caused by an impairment of the 'language switch' (cf. Penfield and Roberts 1959) alleged to be located in the area of the Sylvian fissure. Although this possibility was seriously entertained at one point (cf. Weinreich 1963: 72), a recent comprehensive review of bilingualism and aphasia (Paradis 1977:88-91) found little evidence or need to posit a specifically bilingual switch mechanism localized in the brain.

More recently, studies (Clyne 1967; Lance 1970, 1975; Gumperz and Hernandez-Chavez 1972; Pfaff 1975, 1976, 1979; Timm 1975; Kachru 1978; Lipski 1978; Poplack 1978; Sridhar 1978; Vaid 1980; and others) have shown that intrasentential switching of languages (Code mixing or CM hereafter) is extremely common among bilinguals. In fact, under certain circumstances (e.g., when all the participants in a speech situation share a bilingual background) CM may be the norm rather than the exception. The studies just cited also show that CM is not random but rule-governed and that it is used to achieve a variety of communicative goals, such as, conveying emphasis, verisimilitude, role playing, technical and sociocultural authenticity, and so forth.

The significance of CM for linguistic and psychological research is obvious. CM raises a host of intriguing questions concerning, for example, the rules for permissible and impermissible mixes, the nature of grammatical relationship between the elements of the two languages within the sentence, the interaction of the two rule systems at various stages of sentence production, the implications of CM for the 'single' vs. 'separate' store hypotheses, for the hypothesized 'language switch,' for processing difficulty, and so forth.

Our aim in this study is (a) to present an overview of recent research on the linguistic characteristics of intrasentential CM, and (b) to explore its implications for a psycholinguistic model of bilingual processing. The linguistic description in the first part sets forth what may be called minimal adequacy conditions that must be met by psychological theory. Excepting a few pioneering studies such as Kolers (1966a) and Macnamara and Kushnir (1971), the psycholinguistics of CM is a virgin field, but rich in promise. Hence, any discussion of the issues at this stage in research must necessarily be discursive, indeed, largely speculative, rather than experimental. We do believe, however, that asking the right type of questions may at least constitute a beginning.

## 2. SOME DEFINITIONS

Code mixing refers to the transition from using linguistic units (words, phrases, clauses, etc.) of one language to using those of another within a single sentence. It is to be distinguished from the better known term 'code switching' in two respects: (1) each instance of language alternation in CM is not accompanied by a shift in the speech situation (unlike in the ideal situation described in the quotation from Weinreich, above), and (2) the language alternations take place intra-sententially. CM is also different from borrowing in many ways (1) the mixed elements do not necessarily 'fill lexical gaps' in the host language; (2) the mixed elements are often sequences longer than single words; (3) the mixed elements are not restricted to a more or less limited set accepted by the speech community of the host language--on the contrary, the entire second language system is at the disposal of the code mixer; (4) the mixed elements are not necessarily assimilated into the host language by regular phonological and morphological processes; and finally, as Pfaff (1979:295) rightly observes, (5) the two terms make totally different claims about the competence of the individual speaker: borrowing can occur in monolingual speech, while code mixing is necessarily a product of bilingual competence.

A further set of terms crucial to any discussion of code mixing may be proposed. These refer to the primary language of the discourse (referred to as the **host** language hereafter) and the source language of the mixed elements (the **guest** language). As Wentz (1977) shows, despite extensive mixing of elements from another language, speakers and listeners usually agree on which language is being spoken in a given sentence or discourse.

## 3. CATEGORIES OF ELEMENTS MIXED

Consider the following examples. (The examples cited, except where indicated, come from the present authors' observations of Kannada-English bilingual speech in informal conversations.)

1. nam tande airport-ge hogiddare
   (My father has gone to the airport)

2. avaru committee chairman a:go:du nange iSTa illa
   (I don't like his becoming the committee chairman)

3. And from there I went to live pa' mucho sitios
   (- in a lot of places)
   (Poplack, 1979)

4. El hombre who saw the accident es Cubano
   (the man - is Cuban)
   (Gingras, 1974)

5. The type of work he did cuando trabajaba (when he worked) he . . . what . . . that I remember era regador (he was an irrigator) at that time
   (Gumperz and Hernandez-Chavez, 1972)

6. Fui a cash su cheque
   (I went to cash his check)
   (Pfaff, 1975)

7. No van a bring it up in the meeting
   (They're not going to - )
   (Pfaff, 1975)

8. avaru hi:ge ma:Diya:ru anta I had no idea
   (That he would do this - )

Although elements from practically every syntactic category (including purely grammatical morphemes such as determiners) occur in code mixed sentences, it has been found that certain types of elements are more likely to be mixed than others. In general, except for single words, the higher the constituency of the element, the more likely it is to be mixed: thus, conjoined sentences, main clauses, subordinate clauses (including relative clauses), and major constituents, such as, noun phrases, verb phrases, and prepositional phrases, are among the most frequently mixed elements. Among single words, nouns outrank all others in frequency of mixing, followed by adjectives, adverbs, and verbs. Grammatical items such as articles, quantifiers, auxiliaries, prepositions, and clitics are least likely to be mixed by themselves. For example, in a study based on the recorded speech of Puerto Ricans in New York City, Shana Poplack (1979) found the following distribution of code mixed elements:

**TABLE 7**

*Intra-sentential (Spanish to English) Code Mixing by Syntactic Category (Abstracted from Poplack 1979:45)*

| Syntactic category of mixed elements | No. of mixes | % of total total mixes |
|---|---|---|
| Clauses | 58 | 12 |
| Noun phrases | 103 | 22 |
| Phrases (prep., adj., adv., & infin.) | 39 | 8 |
| Verb phrases | 13 | 3 |
| Single nouns | 141 | 30 |
| Single adjectives | 49 | 11 |
| Single adverbs | 33 | 7 |
| Single verbs | 13 | 3 |
| Conjunctions (subordinate, coordinate, relative pronouns) | 16 | 3 |
| Auxiliary, preposition, determiner | 0 | 0 |
| Total | 465 | |

The observation that certain types of syntactic elements or constituents are more likely to occur in mixed sentences than others is only an indication of the possibility that CM is not a random but a patterned phenomenon. More direct evidence pointing to the existence of a 'grammar of code mixing' comes from a variety of studies, based on the performance of bilingual speakers concerning: (1) judgements of the grammaticality/acceptability of various types of mixed sentences (Lance 1970; Timm 1975; and Wentz 1977); (2) normalizations or regularizations of mixed sentences in repetition tasks (Wentz 1977); and (3) self-corrections in spontaneous speech (Timm 1975).

For example, Gingras (1974) found that members of a bilingual community display an impressive degree of agreement on the judgements of acceptability of code mixed sentences. The following is a sample of sentences judged acceptable by nearly all of Gingras's 38 Chicano informants (the exact percentage of acceptance is given in parentheses).

9 The man que vino ayer (who came yesterday) wants to buy un carro nuevo (a new car). (92%)
10 The hombre viejo (old man) is mad. (90%)
11 El old man esta enojado. (The old man is mad.) (94%)
12 El hombre who saw the accident es Cubano. (The man . . . is Cuban.) (100%)

The informants were equally consistent in rejecting the following sentences as ill-formed.

13 El hombre old esta enojado. (The old man is mad.) (0%)
14 El man old esta enojado. (ibid) (5%)
15 El man viejo esta enojado. (ibid) (5%)
16 El man que came ayer wants John comprar a car nuevo. (The man who came yesterday wants John to buy a new car.) (0%)

The above set of examples shows that we must look beyond probability in explaining the acceptability status of code mixed sentences. Besides the as yet little studied 'stylistic' and 'social meaning' variables, perhaps the most important determinant of acceptability in CM is the structural compatibility of the host and guest language items. We shall take a closer look at this next.

## 4. INTEGRATION OF GUEST ELEMENTS IN HOST STRUCTURES

It might appear at first sight that mixing of single elements such as nouns, verbs, and adjectives is a psycholinguistically simple process. Thus, in the Kannada sentence,

17 Ramu office-ge ho:gida:ne
Ramu office-to gone-has
Ramu has gone to office.

it may be supposed that *office* is substituted for the Kannada word *kacheri*. If this is correct, then mixing of single elements from another language is not different, in principle, from the process involved in the choice between synonyms in the same language, e.g., between *carcinogenic* and *cancer-causing* (cf. Paradis 1977). Even single elements, however, involve much more complex processes of integration than this. Certain lexical items simply cannot be mixed because of restrictions in the host language. A case in point is the impossibility of using *no one* in a sentence in Tamil--or any Dravidian language--because of the absence of the rule attaching the negative to the quantifier in the host language (Annamalai 1971). Thus, while (18) is grammatical, (19) is not:

18 meeting-kku yaarum varale.
Anyone didn't come to the meeting.

19 meeting-kku no one vandaanga.
No one came to the meeting.

Thus the semantic composition necessary for lexical mapping may itself be unavailable.

Even in cases of perfect lexical congruence between the guest item and its host language counterpart (e.g., *blanca* and *white* in Spanish and English), the language-specific constraints on the surface structure placement of the items may bring about structural conflicts. A well known case in point is the placement of Spanish and English adjectives in mixed sentences (Pfaff 1979). Adjectives normally precede the noun in English except in certain specific structures (e.g., when preceded by an adverb) and follow the noun in Spanish except when they are members of a closed set (e.g., possessives, ordinals, and other limiting adjectives). It is interesting to note that when adjectives occur in code mixed sentences, they obey both these constraints. Thus, Spanish adjectives occur preposed in English sentences if they are members of the closed set:

20 mi grandma (my grandmother)
21 el siguiente play (the following play)

And English adjectives occur post-nominally in Spanish if they are preceded by adverbs:

22 **Me lleve chile** ya **roasted** y **peeled...para hecerlo alla.** (I picked up the chile already roasted and peeled for making it there.)

23 ese color como muy **dark** maroon. (that color like very dark maroon).

What this constraint implies, in 'process' terms, is that the speaker monitors the surface structure of the host sentence to ensure its compatability with the structural constraints inherent to the guest item. In other words, not only the lexicons but the entire rule systems of both languages must be simultaneously active in the production of mixed sentences.

Linguists describing code mixed language types have proposed a variety of such substantive constraints to account for the occurrence and non-occurrence of certain types of mixes (Gingras 1974; Gumperz 1970; Kachru 1978; Lipski 1978; McClure & Wentz 1976; Pfaff 1975, 1976, 1979; Poplack 1978, 1979; Sridhar 1978; Timm 1975). The various proposed constraints (e.g., Gumperz's constraint on the mixing of auxiliary verbs, Timm's constraint on the combinability of host finite verbs and guest infinitive complements, and so on) are continually being challenged and modified on the basis of new data (see Wentz 1977; Lipski 1978; and Poplack 1978 for details). While research on such constraints goes on, there does seem to be wide open support for at least one general constraint that subsumes a number of specific constraints suggested earlier. Two versions of this constraint, developed independently by Poplack (1979) and Lipski (1978) are given in 24 and 25 below:

24 *The Equivalence Constraint*: Code switches will tend to occur at points in discourse where juxtaposition of L1 and L2 elements does not violate a syntactic rule of either language i.e., at points around which the surface structures of the two languages map onto each other (Poplack 1979:10-11).

25 *Hypothesis B (informal version)*: Whereas the portion of a code switched utterance that falls before the code switch may indeed contain syntactically divergent elements, those portions falling after the switch must be essentially identical syntactically (Lipski 1978:258).

Although, in our opinion, the two constraints do go a long way toward capturing the essential syntactic principle involved in code mixing, there is, however, one problem shared by both the proposed constraints. This is the lack of specification of the internal constituency of the switched element in Poplack's constraint, and the vagueness associated with the hedge 'essentially' in Lipski's hypothesis. (The hedge is absent from his formal version.) Although she claims that the surface structures of the two languages must map onto each other at the point of the switch, Poplack does not specify what degree of correspondence must obtain for two structures to be considered equivalent. Her example is repeated below as 26:

26 Eng. I told him that so that he would bring it fast
Sp. (yo) le dijje eso pa'que (el) la Trajera lingero
Mixed I told him that PA'que LA trajera LINGERO

Although *told him* and *le dije* on the one hand, and *would bring it* and *la trajera* on the other, are equivalent at a certain level of analysis, they do, of course, differ with regard to the order of elements within the constituents, and to that extent, they are not equivalent. Thus, strictly speaking, the ordering rules in the verb phrase in both the main and the subordinate clause are violated in the mixed sentence.

The problem with Lipski's formulation of the constraint is similar. He used the qualifier 'essentially' with his version of the identity or equivalence constraints because of examples of well-formed mixing where the internal constituency of the mixed element differs from that of its unilingual translation equivalent. Consider his example 17a repeated below as 27:

27 Mixed: No se, porque I never used it.
Eng.: I don't know, because I never used it.
Sp.: No se, porque nunco lo use.

where, except for the placement of the clitic pronoun in Spanish the mixed and the Spanish segments are essentially identical following the switch.

A solution to this problem might be to incorporate into the proposed constraint the Dual Structure Principle first put forward in S. N. Sridhar (1978). A revised version of this principle is given in 28:

28 *Dual structure principle.* The internal structure of the guest constituent need not conform to the constituent structure rules of the host language, so long as its placement in the host sentence obeys the rules of the host language.

Consider the following case. The noun phrase in English consists of a head noun, and optionally, prenominal modifiers such as determiners, adjectives, etc., and post nominal modifiers such as prepositional phrases, relative clauses, sentential complements, etc. In contrast, the noun phrase in Kannada can have only prenominal modifiers, even relative clauses and sentential complements occurring pre-nominally in the language. Now, according to the dual structure principle, English NPs with post-nominal modifiers can be code mixed in Kannada, although they are formed in violation of the constituent structure rules for NPs in Kannada, as long as the English NPs occur in positions normally occupied by NPs in Kannada sentences. This principle is illustrated in the following sentence:

29 avanu obba man of considerable courage.
(He is a man of considerable courage.)

This principle is illustrated even more dramatically in sentence 30:

30 nanna abhipra:yadalli *his visiting her at home* sariyalla
my opinion-in proper not
(In my opinion, his visiting her at home is not proper.)

Consider the italicized segment above with its Kannada counterpart:

30a avanu avalannu mane-yelli noduvudu
he her home-in visiting

Note that the English segment is different from the Kannada version in four important respects: (1) the English subject is marked with possessive ending while the Kannada subject is nominative; (2) the verb precedes the object while the Kannada verb follows its object; (3) the locative is a preposition in English and a postposition in Kannada; and (4) the adverbial phrase (at home) follows the object in English, while it precedes the verb in Kannada. Thus, it is obvious that the internal constituency of the mixed element is autonomously generated by a separate set of rules and that the really crucial constraint concerns only its external relationship with the elements of the host sentence.

## 5. PSYCHOLINGUISTIC IMPLICATIONS

The preceding discussion of some of the major syntactic properties of CM suggests a number of implications for a psychological model of bilingual information processing.

As noted earlier, the focus of psychological research on bilingualism has been the so-called 'linguistic independence' of the bilingual, i.e., his 'feat of separate storage, retrieval, and processing' (Macnamara 1967:67). In order to explain this linguistic independence, Penfield and Roberts (1959) proposed the theory that the neurological mechanisms of the two languages of the bilingual are organized in such a way that when one is on, the other must be off. However, as we have noted above, CM involves simultaneous interaction of the two rule systems in the production of a single sentence. Not only are elements from two languages present in the same sentence, these elements are integrated into a unified syntactic structure by a complex interaction of constraints. Thus, CM requires both systems to be *on* at the same time, thereby rendering unlikely any strong version of the language 'switch' hypothesis.

This conclusion is consistent with a number of recent experimental studies demonstrating interlingual 'interference' or 'facilitation' in bilingual processing (Kolers 1966b; Dalrymple-Alford 1968; Young and Naver 1968 Preston and Lambert 1969; Segalowitz and Lambert 1969; among others.) These studies show that the activation of one language system in the bilingual does not necessarily render the other system inoperative.

Yet, this does not mean that the two systems are 'merged' in the bilingual. After all, even habitual code mixers do produce entirely monolingual discourses in each of their languages when the occasion demands it (e.g., when speaking to a monolingual). Also, even in conversations that seem to be in mixed speech, speakers produce a high proportion of turns speaking entirely in one language or the other (Pfaff 1979:203). The right approach, therefore, seems to be to avoid both the strong linguistic independence model and the merged system model in favor of an *interactionist* model of overlapping systems. The crucial question, of course, is how the overlap is accessed in CM.

The existence of interlingual constraints such as the Equivalence Constraint (and the Dual Structure Principle) seems to indicate the need for positing a comparison stage in the production of mixed utterances (cf. Clyne 1967; Rayfield 1970; Lipski 1978). At this stage the bilingual speaker checks the external patterning or the syntactic compatibility of the guest element with the host sentence. However, it is unlikely that the speaker produces (even subliminally) two entire 'utterances,' one in each language, before making the comparison, as Lipski (1978:263) seems to suggest. Far more likely is the possibility that mixed sentence production involves an *assembly line* process, where individual components (guest constituents) are put together separately and inserted into appropriate slots in the syntactic frame of the host language. It is perhaps only the syntactic constituency of the guest constituents and their external patterning with the host sentence that is checked at the comparison stage.

A very important issue in the psychology of CM is whether CM adds to processing difficulty. Kolers (1966a) found CM to be irrelevant for comprehension but inhibitory for production. A 'switching time' of 0.3-0.5 seconds was found for reading aloud mixed passages, and about 1.3 seconds for free speech and making precis in mixed language. Kolers attributes the longer switching time in the latter conditions to the need to make 'decisions about what to say and about when and how to mix his speech' (p. 372). Macnamara and Kushnir (1971) found a mean switching time for input close to 0.2 seconds in tasks involving silent reading and true/false judgement of visually and orally presented code mixed material. A similar mean switching time of close to 0.2 seconds was found for output in an independent study of number naming by Macnamara, Krauthammer, and Bolgar (1968). All this cumulatively seems to confirm that language switching (or mixing) 'takes an observable amount of time.'

This conclusion must be evaluated in light of the following observation: in the mixed passages employed in the Kolers study, words were 'haphazardly in English or French, half the passages favoring English word order and the other half favoring French' (Kolers 1966a:358). It is possible, therefore, that the extra processing time was due, in part at least, to the ungrammaticality of (some of) the sentences (i.e., in terms of the norms of CM). This criticism applies equally to the Macnamara and Kushnir study, because some of their passages were those used in Kolers' study, and the others also seem to have been put together rather mechanically. However, this does not explain the strong evidence for switching time found by Kolers in the 'free speech' condition.

Assuming that this observed switching time may be replicated in other naturalistic sentence processing tasks with appropriate syntactic controls, it is interesting to speculate further on the extent and cause of the extra processing time. First of all, the switching time of approximately .20 seconds is, as Macnamara, Krauthammer, and Bolgar (1968) observe, little over the minimum threshold of speed for language operations observed by Lenneberg (1967). Second, as the same authors note, the more regular the switch, the less time it takes, and there is evidence that CM is a rule governed phenomenon, although the rules have only just begun to be discovered. Third, Kolers (1966a) found that practice reduces switching time, and CM is a stable, habitual mode of language use --a full-fledged code in the bilingual's repertoire like any other code. These considerations suggest that the processing difficulty involved in code mixed sentences may be very small, even if real.

The preceding discussion of switching refers, of course, to what Kolers has called the 'phonological' switching time (and the corresponding 'auditory' switching time in comprehension). It will be recalled that the actual switching time in free speech was much greater, an increase attributed by Kolers to the 'cognitive cost of switching' (p. 365). A factor contributing to this cognitive cost may be the Dual Structure Principle, requiring interaction of two separate sets of syntactic rules in the production of the same sentence.

Another interesting issue in the psycholinguistics of CM is the status of mixed elements as units in sentence planning. An attractive hypothesis abut sentence planning is that the 'idea' or the message underlying a sentence is put together in chunks of various sizes or degrees of complexity, each chunk functioning as a unit at a particular level (cf. S. N. Sridhar, 1988). Transitions from one language to another, then, could occur between chunks. Thus, it is intuitively appealing to consider noun phrases, relative clauses, subordinate clauses of all kinds, prepositional phrases, and so on (or, strictly speaking, the 'meaning' of such constituents) as 'good' chunks--or internally coherent thought units--whereas certain other combinations would not so qualify, e.g., two function words, a preposition and an article. This could be translated into testable predictions about (a) what kinds of elements and combinations would be mixed, and (b) what kinds of mixing would be comprehended faster.

In the only relevant study in this area, Kolers (1966a) found that the majority of prepositional phrases in mixed spoken precis were unilingual, but if the unit were mixed, article and noun were more likely to be in the same language than preposition and article. This seems to suggest that while a prepositional phrase may be a syntactic unit, a noun phrase may be a more basic conceptual unit. However, in the next task (reading aloud of mixed passages), Kolers found subjects invariably 'translating' elements of prepositional phrases into the language of the immediately preceding word, either within that unit or outside of it. This produced some cases where the preposition and article were in one language, and the noun in the other, leading Kolers to conclude that there is no linguistic unit larger than the word whose boundaries are not permeable. Two observations may be made about this conclusion. First, the 'interference' due to contiguity observed in the second task may be specific to reading, and may not be generalizable to spontaneous speech. Therefore, the permeability of syntactic boundaries in reading aloud may not be conclusive evidence regarding their status as 'thought units' in sentence production. Second, Kolers analyzed the data from the perspective of the host language--and the integrity of its constituent structure boundaries. It would be equally interesting to examine the internal structure of the guest segments, to see whether they can be considered 'thought units.' A number of constraints against the mixing of single function words, such as determiners (Gumperz and Hernandez-Chavez 1972), conjunctions (Kachru 1978), auxiliaries (Timm 1975), and others, have been proposed, which, if they survive the attacks on the basis of putative counter-examples, would support the usefulness of exploring the status of the mixed elements as representing units of thought.

## 6. CONCLUSION

We have tried to show in this paper that Code Mixing is an exciting and promising field of research both in syntax and psycholinguistics, and especially when the two orientations interact. Besides its acknowledged sociolinguistic importance, this phenomenon raises a host of intriguing issues, such as defining cross-linguistic formal and functional equivalence, universal constraints on mixability of categories and structures, the mental representation and interaction of cognitive systems, the processing complexity of bilingual performance, and the psychological status of linguistic structures as thought units, among others.

As noted already, much of this study has been speculative. This is unavoidable, given (1) the almost total neglect of CM by psychologists, and (2) the rather primitive nature of current psycholinguistic models of bilingual information processing. It is no exaggeration to say that, except in the couple of studies discussed above, syntax has been a stranger to the psychology of bilingualism. The experimental paradigms have been either naive (indiscriminate mixture of elements from two languages) or quaint (reciting the alphabet backwards). The pressing need in psycholinguistic research on bilingualism is the study of sentential processing, designed with adequate syntactic controls. Preferably, such studies should involve languages that are typologically different from one another. The study of Code Mixing is an area where such paradigms and controls are not only desirable but essential.

# Chapter 7

# English in a South Indian Urban Context

## 1. INTRODUCTION

This paper discusses the use of English vis-a-vis Hindi and the mother tongue (Kannada) in the state of Karnataka in South India. My discussion is based on the results of an empirical survey involving university students and employees in public and private sectors. The results of this survey, a pilot project though it was, are interesting and important in three respects. First, this is one of few empirical studies of the language situation in Karnataka in particular, and in India in general. Second, it helps us understand the complementarity of role distribution among languages in a multilingual society. And third, it helps us assess the degree of success of institutional efforts in language planning in India.

## 2. BACKGROUND

There have been a number of studies examining the role of different languages in multilingual societies and on language choice among bilinguals. Greenfield and Fishman (1971) discuss the roles of Spanish and English in the Puerto Rican community in New York City. Spanish is associated with values such as intimacy and solidarity and is used primarily in domains such as family and friendship, while English is associated with values such as differentiation and is used in domains such as religion, education, and employment. We can thus distinguish between what may be termed "affective" and "utilitarian" domains.

Cooper and Carpenter's "Linguistic Diversity in the Ethiopian Market" (1972) is an extensive study of languages used in twenty-three Ethiopian markets. There is no evidence that Amharic, Arabic, or any other language has emerged as a lingua franca for trade. The authors conclude by observing that in the linguistically diverse contexts of these Ethiopian markets, transactions were facilitated by the traders' multilingualism, rather than by the emergence of a trade lingua franca.

Ferguson's study, entitled "The Role of Arabic in Ethiopia" (1970) deals with Arabic in relation to English, Amharic, and French. Ferguson's emphasis is slightly different from that of the present study in that he is concerned primarily with Ethiopians' attitudes toward the possible roles of the various languages, rather than with the distribution of these languages in various domains. Ferguson's research technique is similar to the present one, however, in using a questionnaire for gathering data.

Whiteley's *Language in Kenya* (1974) reports the results of an extensive survey of language usage in multilingual Kenya. The situation he describes bears many interesting parallels to that of India. In Kenya, a number of factors have contributed to a situation in which the use of a particular language has come to be characteristic of a particular social domain, in much the same way that domains are characterized in England by varieties of English. The languages themselves have taken on the complex of emotions, prestige, etc., associated with the domains. Local languages like Kamba or Kipsigis may be linked with the rural homestead or with traditional values; Swahili may be linked with town life, trade, and certain kinds of jobs; English is associated with government service, the professions, and high-status jobs.

Most germane to the present study are the linguistic surveys conducted by Pandit (1978) and Kachru (1976). Pandit's "Language and Identity: The Panjabi Language in Delhi" reports the results of a questionnaire survey administered to undergraduate students of a women's college in New Delhi. The data indicates the relative usage of English, Panjabi, and Hindi in affective domains (domestic, neighborhood, religion) as well as in utilitarian ones (e.g., education, mass media, reading and writing) by Hindu, Sikh, and Muslim students. Pandit's data indicate the relatively higher usage of English in utilitarian domains, and of the mother tongue in affective domains.

Kachru's study deals with the use of English among the student and faculty of English departments in Indian universities. This study also used the questionnaire method, and part of it deals with the use of English in some selected domains. Although Kachru's study indicated a preference for English in what is termed utilitarian domains, these results, by virtue of the circumstances in which the study was conducted, have some limitations. First, the population consisted of people professionally committed to the use of English. Second, the population was drawn mainly from large metropolitan areas such as Bombay, Delhi, Madras, and Hyderabad. Third, the questions did not involve a comparison between English and other languages in different domains. Finally, no correlational analysis was made; hence a finer isolation of variables has not been possible.

## 3. THE PRESENT STUDY

The present study is an expansion of Kachru's, more limited in some respects and broader in others. It is limited in the sense that only one Indian state in involved; also, no attempt is made to elicit attitudes toward the different varieties of English, or to determine what role languages should play in India. However, it is broader in that it represents both student and worker populations; the former includes students from a variety of disciplines (excluding English literature). Within the worker population, a wide variety of occupations is represented. Therefore the results of this study complement Kachru's.

My data come from two questionnaires administered to two distinct populations in the summer of 1977.[3] The first set of subjects consisted of undergraduate students studying for the degrees of Bachelor of Arts, Bachelor of Science, or Bachelor of Commerce in four private colleges, two in the state capital and semi-metropolitan city of Bangalore, and two in the medium-sized city of Shimoga. A second questionnaire was administered to public and private sector employees in Bangalore. This population consisted of (1) white-collar employees of the Karnataka Government Insurance Department; (2) federal government employees of the Indian Posts and Telegraphs Department in the General Post Office in Bangalore; (3) employees of the Life Insurance Corporation of India - a nationwide (public sector) undertaking; (4) employees of the Public Works Department (engineering division) of the Government of Karnataka; and (5) employees of a prosperous private engineering consultant firm. This population included both highly educated and skilled professionals and middle-level employees.

The student questionnaire dealt with the following topics: demographic data; fields of specialization; their choice of the current and previous medium of instruction, and reasons for the choice; educational level and occupation of parents; languages in which the students claimed competence and their degrees of competence; job aspirations of the students; preference for English, Hindi, or mother tongue in the following domains: (1) mass media (radio, newspapers, and magazines) and (2) a number of interpersonal situations. This last category specified the following: with family, friends, teachers, neighbors; with relatives at marriages and socio-religious functions; with office or bank employees; while discussing politics, technical topics, etc., and while visiting another state in India. The rationale for eliciting all these different kinds of data was that each factor might be a significant variable affecting patterns of language choice. The second questionnaire involved roughly the same demographic data, except information was also gathered about the subjects' occupations and incomes, and the domains concentrated on occupational interaction (while talking with colleagues and superiors, with subordinate staff, with public customers, etc.).

A total of 299 students and 88 employees responded to the questionnaire. Analysis of the responses reveals very interesting patterns of language usage.

## 4. RESULTS

I will first discuss the responses of students (4.1-4.3) and then discuss the responses of the employees.

### 4.1 Medium of Instruction, Job Prospects, and Upward Mobility

First, let us look at the percentage of students who preferred English to their mother tongue as the medium of instruction at the high school level. Although this choice was available to all the students, 68 percent chose English, 27 percent mother tongue, and only 5 percent other languages, including Hindi/Urdu. The reasons for this choice become apparent when we analyze the students' response to another question: "What will be your opportunities if your education was through (1) English, (2) Hindi-Urdu, (3) mother tongue, or (4) the state language?" The responses are given in Table 8.

**TABLE 8**

*Job Prospects and the Language of Training (%)*

| Languages | None | Good | Very Good | Excellent | No Ans. |
|---|---|---|---|---|---|
| English | 1 | 20 | 16 | 52 | 11 |
| Hindi/Urdu | 18 | 20 | 7 | 0 | 45 |
| Mother Tongue | 8 | 20 | 12 | 16 | 44 |
| State Language | 20 | 11 | 6 | 3 | 60 |

The majority (52 percent) said that their job prospects would be excellent if their education was through English; the mother tongue placed a very distinct second. No student felt the same way about Hindi/Urdu; indeed, 18 percent thought their job prospects would be nil with Hindi/Urdu. This preference for English is consistent with the educational goals and job preferences of the respondents: 85 percent indicated a desire to pursue a master's degree or higher; as for job preference, 31 percent wanted to become bank managers, 15 percent college or university teachers, 14 percent high-level officers in the Indian Administrative Service, and 10 percent lawyers. These educational goals and preferences reflect the ubiquitous desire for upward mobility. (The educational level of the parents of 81 percent of students is a B.A. degree or lower.)

## 4.2 Claimed Proficiency in Language

Let us now turn to the question of language competence. Table 9 presents the percentage of students who claim proficiency in the languages specified below in various domains.

**TABLE 9**

*Students Claiming Proficiency in Various Languages (%)*

| Language | Proficiency<br>None | Enough for most conversations |
|---|---|---|
| English | - | 29 |
| Hindi/Urdu | 19 | 11 |
| Mother Tongue | - | 63 |
| State language (if other than mother tongue) | - | 18 |

Next to the mother tongue, the language in which most people claim proficiency is English (nearly 30 percent); as many as 19 percent claim no proficiency in Hindi/Urdu. These results throw much light on the sociolinguistic status of English compared to Hindi/Urdu in South India. It is a well-known sociolinguistic phenomenon that when a language commands prestige in a society, even those who have minimal or marginal proficiency in that language are eager to claim to know it; for example, it is very common in India to find even those who have had only four to six weeks' instruction in French or German listing it among the languages they know. The poor showing of Hindi/Urdu vis-a-vis English correctly reflects the attitudinal barrier that Hindi must overcome in the South before it can claim to be a pan-Indian language.

## 4.3 The Use of English, Mother Tongue, and Hindi-Urdu

Now to turn to the actual use of English, mother tongue, and Hindi/Urdu in Karnataka. The first domain we shall consider is the mass media--newspapers and radio. The response to the question of the language of the printed media is given in Table 10.

### 4.3.1 *Language Use in the Print Media*

The readership of English-language newspapers is slightly more than that of Indian-language newspapers, whereas the readership of English and Indian-language magazines is about equal. This confirms the common observation that the educated Indians rely largely on English-language newspapers and magazines for state and local news and for light general reading, respectively. Unfortunately, the table does not give a language-by-language breakdown of the Indian-language newspapers and magazines. However, the respondents did list the periodicals they regularly read; from this it is clear that most periodicals are in Kannada and other regional languages, and that the role of Hindi/Urdu in this domain is marginal.

**TABLE 10**

*Students who read English and Indian Language Daily Newspapers and Magazines (%)*

| | Number of periodicals read | | | | | |
|---|---|---|---|---|---|---|
| | 1 | 2 | 3 | 4 | 5 | above 5 |
| English language newspapers | 56 | 14 | 10 | - | - | 20 |
| Indian language newspapers | 50 | 12 | 7 | 1 | 1 | 29 |
| English language magazines | 30 | 14 | 17 | 4 | 1 | 34 |
| Indian language magazines | 29 | 21 | 19 | 3 | 1 | 27 |

It is interesting to contrast the pattern of English use in this domain with that reported in Kachru's (1976) study. Kachru found that as many as 71 percent of the respondents "always" read newspapers and magazines in English; in my study, the figure is 56 percent. For general reading, Kachru's figure was 64 percent; mine is only 30 percent. The difference may be attributed to the fact that Kachru's subjects were all students majoring in English literature, whereas my subject population is more diversified. Nevertheless, the percentage of students reading newspapers and magazines in English in the present sample remains extremely impressive, testifying to the powerful role of English in the mass media.

### 4.3.2 *Language Use on the Radio*

The next question referred to the language of radio news broadcasts. Seventeen percent of the students claimed to listen to English-language newscasts exclusively, and 16 percent to newscasts in the mother tongue exclusively. As many as 61 percent claimed to listen to both. A high percentage of these latter responses may be explained by the fact that 88 percent of the students' mothers had an educational level of matriculation (secondary school) or less; in such families it is typical for both English and the mother tongue to be used.

### 4.3.3 *Language Use in the Interpersonal Domain*

The use of languages in interpersonal domains is summarized in Table 11. These domains may be broadly divided into two classes: the intimate or affective domains (items A-D) and the formal or utilitarian ones (items E-I). As predicted, in intimate domains the language(s) used regularly are the mother tongue and English, in that order. The language most rarely used is Hindi/Urdu.

One interesting result might be worth noting: while there is a big gap between the use of English and the mother tongue in most of the intimate domains, the gap is very narrow when it comes to interaction with friends. This may be due to shared educational status, goals and interests.

Turning to the formal or utilitarian domains, one finds that English is consistently preferred over the mother tongue and Hindi/Urdu. The preference for English when interacting with teachers shows that English is still very much the language of higher education; it also probably reflects the fact that the mother tongue lacks the technical registers used in academic discussions. (The negligible difference between the use of English and the mother tongue for political and technical discussions is almost certainly due to a defect in the testing instrument. If I had separated political from technical discussion, I am sure the pattern of response would have been quite different. Politics is discussed informally in India, and lexical borrowings in the regional languages make the code adequate for this function. Technical discussion, on the other hand, more often results in code switching, since code mixing is not adequate).

TABLE 11

*Students who use Mother Tongue, English and Hindi/Urdu in Social Interaction*

| Domain | | Language | Regularly | Rarely |
|---|---|---|---|---|
| A. | Family | English | 15 | 29 |
| | | Mother Tongue | 87 | 1 |
| | | Hindi/Urdu | 3 | 54 |
| B. | Friends | English | 42 | 8 |
| | | Mother Tongue | 53 | 12 |
| C. | Neighbors who can speak your languag | English | 17 | 24 |
| | | Mother Tongue | 65 | 6 |
| | | Hindi/Urdu | 4 | 48 |
| D. | Friends & relatives, during weddings, etc. | English | 24 | 15 |
| | | Mother Tongue | 71 | 3 |
| | | Hindi/Urdu | 5 | 47 |
| E. | Teachers | English | 57 | 3 |
| | | Mother Tongue | 24 | 26 |
| | | Hindi/Urdu | 2 | 57 |
| F. | Strangers on the bus | English | 47 | 11 |
| | | Mother Tongue | 35 | 11 |
| | | Hindi/Urdu | 5 | 48 |
| G. | Office and bank employees | English | 57 | 8 |
| | | Mother Tongue | 26 | 17 |
| | | Hindi/Urdu | 2 | 49 |
| H. | Political & technical discussions | English | 42 | 8 |
| | | Mother Tongue | 41 | 12 |
| | | Hindi/Urdu | 4 | 50 |
| I. | While visiting another state in India | English | 64 | 6 |
| | | Mother Tongue | 17 | 27 |
| | | Hindi/Urdu | 15 | 32 |

Proceeding next to the domain of interaction with office and bank employees, we again notice a preference for English. This may be due to two factors. First, despite the efforts of state and central governments, English is still very much the language of administration. Second, English is felt to be the language of power, a language of prestige. By and large, it is easier to get things done in a government office or a bank if one speaks English than if one speaks the mother tongue. Again, notice the poor showing of Hindi/Urdu in this domain.

Finally, consider the responses under Item I, which show the roles of English, Hindi/Urdu, and the mother tongue as interstate link languages. Again English is preferred, and the frequency of mother tongue use goes down, not unexpectedly; but what is interesting is the considerably better rating of Hindi/Urdu--for the first time the figures are in double digits. The 15 percent rating of Hindi/Urdu does not compare with the 64 percent rating of English as link language; furthermore, the rating given to Hindi/Urdu would probably be given to any other regional language, if the question had specified the state where the language was spoken. This hypothesis is confirmed by the fact that the rating for Hindi/Urdu actually remains lower than that of the mother tongue.

The preceding discussion demonstrates a clear and identifiable pattern of language distribution in various domains. The mother tongue is dominant in intimate or affective domains, whereas in formal or utilitarian ones the language of choice is English. All the functions investigated in this study are adequately (and most exhaustively) handled by the mother tongue and English. Hindi/Urdu plays a very marginal role.

#### 4.3.4 *Language Use by Employees*

When comparing the patterns of language use by students with those of employees (see Table 12), again we note the clear preference for the mother tongue in the intimate domain (66%). In domain B and E--that is, with colleagues and superiors, and with customers who do not speak the respondents' mother tongue–the preference is again overwhelmingly for English. The response in Item C is very interesting; with subordinate staff (which in the context of this survey must refer, by and large, to clerks and "attenders") the roles of the languages are reversed: English is used least (probably only with clerks and typists), and the mother tongue most frequently (48%). Hindi/Urdu is used more in this domain than in any other. The relative ranking of the three languages is a good indicator of their status in the attitudinal hierarchy. There is one apparently puzzling result under Item D, however: as many as 27 percent of the respondents claim to use Hindi/Urdu in this domain, although the number of respondents with Hindi/Urdu as their mother tongue is only 2 percent.

TABLE 12

*Employees who use English, Mother Tongue, and Hindi/Urdu in Professional Contexts (%)*

| Domain | | Language | Regularly | Rarely |
|---|---|---|---|---|
| A. | Friends | English | 33 | 6 |
| | | Mother Tongue | 66 | 3 |
| | | Hindi/Urdu | 25 | 6 |
| B. | Colleagues & superiors | English | 64 | 3 |
| | | Mother Tongue | 31 | 19 |
| | | Hindi/Urdu | 16 | 7 |
| C. | Subordinate staff | English | 22 | 25 |
| | | Mother Tongue | 48 | 14 |
| | | Hindi/Urdu | 30 | 5 |
| D. | Customers who speak mother tongue | English | 38 | 9 |
| | | Mother Tongue | 45 | 13 |
| | | Hindi/Urdu | 27 | 6 |
| E. | Customers who don't speak your language | English | 74 | 1 |
| | | Mother Tongue | 5 | 25 |
| | | Hindi/Urdu | 14 | 14 |

This last finding is consistent with another very general effect noticed in the employees' responses. Although Hindi/Urdu is used less frequently than English and the mother tongue in most formal domains, it is nevertheless used more frequently by employees than by students. This may be due in part to two factors: first, only about half of the employees claim to know Kannada (including 43 percent who are native speakers); second, most respondents are employed in nation-wide public or private enterprises and hold transferable jobs. It is clear that Hindi/Urdu is perceived as better suited than English to serve as a low-level lingua franca.

Summarizing the finding from the employees' responses, we see that, as with the students, the mother tongue is used primarily in the intimate domain; English is the language of choice in professional contexts, except with subordinate staff; English is also the preferred language with customers when there is no shared language; and Hindi is the language of interaction with subordinate staff, after the mother tongue.

## 5. CONCLUSION

I believe the data and analysis presented here give us a clear, empirically based picture of language use and language attitudes in a developing multilingual society. The findings confirm the recurrent pattern of use of the mother tongue in intimate or affective domains. These data also provide strong empirical evidence to support the claims made about the role of English in present-day India (e.g., Sridhar 1977) We have seen its importance in the domains of the mass media, academic and professional interaction, administration, and interstate communication. We have also seen its power and prestige in terms of job opportunities. In contrast, the mother tongue and Hindi/Urdu are less versatile. Hindi/Urdu in particular seems to be of marginal communicative value for students and employees in Karnataka.

All these findings "make sense" when viewed in light of what Kachru (1976) has called the pragmatic role hierarchy in the multilingual's repertoire. In this model, the position of a given language in the multilingual's language hierarchy is determined by very pragmatic considerations. The more roles a language can open up for the speaker, the higher its position. Students and professionals in Karnataka feel that English equips them for the largest number of socially valued roles; next comes the mother tongue. As of the date of this study (1977), efforts of propagandists for Hindi, including the federal government, have not succeeded in translating a constitutional mandate into a pragmatic reality for the people of South India. It would be interesting to sample a comparable population at a later date to identify the changes in patterns of multilingual behavior.

# Chapter 8

# Pragmatic Features of Indigenized Varieties:
## Requesting in Indian English

### 1. INTRODUCTION

Recent research on language use attempts to cover "all the contextual coordinates of language organization", to use Levinson's terms (1983). One contextual parameter that has attracted a great deal of attention has been the Speech Act theory (Austin 1962, Searle 1964). As Levinson points out (1983:226), psychologists have proposed that the acquisition of the concepts underlying speech acts may be a prerequisite for language acquisition in general (see, e.g., Bruner 1975, Bates 1976), and psycholinguists have extended the applicability of the notion of speech acts to second language acquisition (see, e.g., Jakobovits and Gordon 1974, Wolfson and Judd 1983).

In studies of indigenized varieties of English (hereafter IVE's), with few exceptions (D'Souza 1987, Kachru 1982b, 1983a, 1986, Smith 1983), not much attention has been paid to what may be called the pragmatic aspects of variation. By pragmatic aspects, I mean topics such as how certain speech acts, such as informatives, directives, commissives, etc., are performed in these varieties. Since IVE's differ from native varieties in the performance of speech acts as well as in formal properties, it is possible that the pragmatic approach may succeed in capturing the uniqueness of an IVE where structural analyses fail to do so.

Recent studies have shown that there are important cross-cultural and cross-linguistic differences in the way the "same" speech act is performed in different languages. For example,

Olshtain and Cohen (1983) have pointed out that an apology in Hebrew is less likely to include a "promise of forbearance" or "an offer of repair" (for the damage) that is there in English. They also observe that the two languages differ in both the range of offenses for which an apology is offered and the intensity of the expression of regret. (For other cross-cultural differences see Apte 1974a, Loveday 1982, Sridhar and Sridhar 1986, and Wolfson and Judd 1983, among others). As we shall see, pragmatic differences exist between varieties of the same language as well, especially between native and non-native varieties, and between one non-native variety and another. It is perhaps useful to remind ourselves at the outset that the study of language variation and change in an IVE involves, by definition: (1) a *cross-cultural comparison* between native and indigenized varieties; (2) a *bilingual's competence* in the English language, with the first language and culture playing an important role; and (3) a range or *continuum of competence* in a second language.

## 2. DESIGN OF THE STUDY

In this study I will focus on requesting as a speech act, and examine how Indian English speakers perform this speech act. The study is based on an analysis of 1148 examples of "request" expressions collected in Bangalore, India, in January 1988, using an elicitation technique in which college students were asked to provide "free responses to structured situations" (cf. Olshtain and Cohen 1983) given to them in the form of a questionnaire.[4]

The questionnaire given to the students was divided into three parts. Part I elicited background information on the students' native language, area of study, earlier training and exposure to English, use of English, mother tongue and the regional language in the various utilitarian and affective domains, and how comfortable they felt using English. Part II outlined seven discourse situations and asked them to write down what they would say to request the service, favor, etc., specified in each situation. The situations were constructed so as to incorporate a number of socio-cultural variables, such as, deference, Westernized versus traditional (South Indian) setting, differences in social status between the requestor and the requestee, etc. In Part III, the respondents indicated whether they would use their mother tongue, English, or both languages in each of the seven situations presented in Part II. All responses were in writing. The requesting expressions were analyzed in relation to (1) the sociocultural variables incorporated in the stimulus situations; (2) the socio-cultural background of the students themselves; and (3) the conventions governing the performance of the speech act in English and the conventions governing the performance of equivalent speech acts in their own languages. The characteristics of the language used by the Indian students were compared to the way requests are performed in a native variety of English, namely American English, as revealed in the judgments and comments on the acceptability of students' responses by two native speakers of American English who were experienced teachers of English as a second language.

One hundred and sixty-four second year undergraduate students from three different colleges (Mount Carmel College, NMRV College and Vijaya College) in the cosmopolitan city of Bangalore, South India (population: over 3 million), took part in the study. The students all came from what is roughly described as a "middle class" background in India. However, their socio-cultural backgrounds were interestingly varied. Students from Mount Carmel College (MCC hereafter) typically came from more Westernized family and friendship backgrounds. These students tend to have greater facility in spoken English, having studied through the English medium practically from Kindergarten and also having attended 'convent' schools where the use of the child's mother tongue is usually discouraged. Students from Vijaya College (VC, hereafter), on the other hand, come from a relatively more "traditional" background, with their culture rooted in the regional language, Kannada, in the case of the majority of the students. Students from the third campus, NMRV College (NMRVC, hereafter) may be said to be somewhat in between the two clearly defined poles, though they may be closer to MCC than to VC.

The study tested two hypotheses: (1) whether the differences in socio-cultural background affected the choice of verbal strategies in requesting: in the choice of language in a neutral encounter, in the choice of address forms, and in the choice of syntactic and semantic formulae and lexical items; (2) whether the students from the more Westernized background (e.g., MCC students) would perform requests in a more native- (English) like manner, while those from traditional backgrounds (e.g., VC students) would use strategies more closely reflecting those of Indian languages, with those from NMRVC falling in-between.

The breakdown of the students from the three colleges is as follows: NMRVC 65; MCC 49; and VC 50. The mother tongues of the students are given in Table 13. The majority of the students (73%) are speakers of the four major Dravidian languages of South India--Kannada, the major language of the state of Karnataka, of which Bangalore is the capital; Malayalam, Tamil, and Telugu--and of Hindi-Urdu. The other languages represented are Konkani, Gujarati, Sindhi, Marathi, Punjabi, and Tulu.

TABLE 13

*Mother Tongues of Students*

| *Language* | *No. of Speakers* | *Percentage* |
|---|---|---|
| Kannada | 59 | 36.0 |
| Tamil | 30 | 18.3 |
| Telugu | 25 | 15.2 |
| Hindi/Urdu | 20 | 12.2 |
| Konkani | 8 | 4.9 |
| Malayalam | 6 | 3.7 |
| Others | 16 | 9.7 |
| | 164 | 100 |

For almost all the students (97%), English was the medium of instruction at high school and college levels. In other words, they had studied English for *at least 6 years.* Many had studied English as a subject and the other subjects through the medium of English much longer. (However, as we shall see, having English as medium of instruction means different things in different settings.) Ninety percent of the students claimed that they used English most often with their friends. An even higher number (98%) claimed that they felt comfortable using English. (This claim turned out to be interesting in the light of the data analyzed below; see especially discussion of situation 2). These claims reflect not only the multilingual, cosmopolitan nature of Bangalore city where English often serves as a link language, but also the fact that it is prestigious to claim competence in English.

## 3. RESULTS AND DISCUSSION

I shall now turn to a detailed discussion of the requesting strategies reported by the students. The various types of constructions used for each of the seven situations will be summarized in table form, in which the most frequently given response types along with the number and percentage of subjects who chose these response types will be given. I will discuss the other, less common responses only when they illustrate a noteworthy aspect of the socio-cultural context (i.e., those considered to be particularly "deviant" or unusual by the two native speaker judges).

***Situation #1:*** *You are visiting your friend's house. Your friend is busy inside. Her/His mother comes out and asks you to sit down. You are very thirsty and need a glass of water. How would you ask her for a glass of water?*

One of the features of the responses noted by native English speakers was the students' use of address forms. In Indian languages, it is customary to address elders with a kinship term. The addressee's proper name with title (e.g., Mrs. Waverly) is never used. (It would be considered "uppity" or disrespectful.) With one's own relatives, the first name is often used with the kinship term (e.g., "Aunt Grace," as in American English). In the given situation, the friend's mother was addressed as "aunty" by 92 out of a total of 164 (or 56.1%) respondents. Native speakers of English found the use of 'aunty' strange. However, it is worthy of note that 'aunty' is an English word grafted on to a basically Indic semantic pattern, which functions as a marker of Westernized sophistication among the upwardly mobile middle classes in urban and semi-urban India. This is seen clearly in the distribution of the use of 'aunty' in the three colleges (see Table 14): it is most frequently used by NMRVC students (64%) and MCC students (57.1%) and least by VC students (46%).

**TABLE 14**

***Distribution of 'Aunty'***

| *College* | *No. of respondents* | *No. of subjects using Aunty* | *%* |
|---|---|---|---|
| Mount Carmel | 49 | 28 | 57.1 |
| NMRV College | 65 | 41 | 63.7 |
| Vijaya College | 50 | 23 | 46.0 |
| Total | 164 | 92 | 56.1 |

I will now analyze the choice of syntactic and semantic formulae used in this situation. The responses (see Table 15) may be grouped into two types--those that involved questions and those that did not. Of course, the former is the preferred, polite pattern of request in native varieties of English. Questions are used for requesting in Indian languages, but that is not the only polite strategy. It is quite acceptable in Indian languages to use polite imperatives or desideratives as requests, especially since the force of the imperative is "toned down" by honorific number-marking on the verb and by the use of non-peremptory intonation (see, e.g., S. N. Sridhar 1989).

TABLE 15

***Choice of Formulae in Requesting Water***

| *Constructions* | *MCC* | *%* | *NMRVC* | *%* | *VC* | *%* |
|---|---|---|---|---|---|---|
| Imperatives<br>*Please give . . .*<br>*Give/Get me . . .* | 3 | 6.1 | 8 | 12.3 | 13 | 26.0 |
| Permission<br>*Can/could/may I have* | 41 | 83.8 | 49 | 75.4 | 22 | 44.0 |
| Ability/Willingness<br>*Can/could/ you get*<br>*Will/would you get* | 3 | 6.1 | 5 | 7.7 | 5 | 10.0 |
| Desiderative<br>*I like/want/need . . .* | 1 | 2.0 | 3 | 4.6 | 5 | 10.0 |
| Bare Nominal<br>*Glass of water* | 0 | -- | 0 | -- | 3 | 6.0 |
| Other | 1 | 2.0 | 0 | -- | 1 | 2.0 |
| Request in native lg. | | | | | | |
| Invalid | 0 | -- | 0 | -- | 1 | 2.0 |
| Total | 49 | 100 | 65 | 100 | 50 | 100 |

The overwhelming majority of the students, 125 out of 164 (76%) used indirect questions involving permission, ability, or willingness, much like native speakers would use in this situation. However, as many as 33 (20%) used imperatives or desideratives, reflecting Indian language conventions. The use of imperatives and desideratives was more characteristic of VC students, and constituted more than a third of their responses, while these patterns accounted for only 8% of MCC responses and 16% of NMRVC requests.[5]

It is also interesting to note that even the students of MCC, who are relatively more native-like in their English, express politeness in ways that are not used in native English. A case in point is the fact that as many as 13 out of 49 students (26.5%) used "please" sentence-initially with indirect questions ("Please, could I have a glass of water?")--a usage that seems to convey importunation rather than just politeness in native usage.

Unexpectedly, two students actually wrote their responses in Kannada, the main local language. While it is easy to dismiss such responses as aberrant, I think that would be a mistake. What such responses indicate is that English is not always appropriate for many types of transactions in a bilingual society and that these students were being more "true to life" in giving a Kannada response in such situations. This phenomenon underscores the complementarity of functions performed by the various languages in the linguistic repertoire of bilinguals (see chapter 4).

***Situation #2:*** *You are in the local Koshy's restaurant with some friends. You want to order some snacks. How would you ask the waiter for the menu?*

This situation tested the effect of two variables: one was the Westernized setting, and the other the relatively low socio-economic status of the addressee. In contrast with the traditional restaurants, where the waiter, a rather low-status employee (often a teenager) orally recites the menu at the patron's table, Koshy's is a fashionable restaurant in the Westernized part of Bangalore, "the Cantonment". The choice of various formulae in this situation (see Table 16, next page) reveals fascinating differences among the three groups of students, and gives us insights into the powerful role of socio-cultural factors in the choice of request strategies.

First of all, note that only about one half of the respondents, (84/163 or 51.5%) chose indirect questions. As many as 35 (21.4%) employed imperatives. And another 24 (14.7%) used a bare nominal ("menu, please"), while 15 (9%) actually placed the order rather than request the menu. The significant frequency of the use of these (non-question) patterns suggests that despite the Westernized setting of the restaurant, the low social status associated with the waiter in traditional restaurants plays a role in the choice of request strategies. This is particularly so in the case of students from VC, where as many as one third of the students (17 or 35%) used imperatives and a much smaller number (13 or 26%) used indirect requests. It is worth noting that almost one fourth of the VC students actually placed the order rather than ask for the menu, following the practice in traditional restaurants. Here, as in the previous situation, we find that the students from MCC are nearer to native English norms, and VC students are closer to their mother tongue norms (see note).

TABLE 16

*Choice of Formulae in Requesting Menu*

| *Constructions* | *MCC* | *%* | *NMRVC* | *%* | *VC* | *%* |
|---|---|---|---|---|---|---|
| Imperatives<br>*Get/give me/us . . .*<br>*Let me/us have . . .*<br>*Show us the . . .* | 8 | 16.3 | 10 | 15.6 | 17 | 34.0 |
| Possibility<br>*Can/could/may we/*<br>*I have* | 30 | 61.2 | 32 | 50.0 | 13 | 26.0 |
| Ability/Willingness<br>Can you bring/get | 3 | 6.1 | 6 | 9.4 | 0 | -- |
| Desiderative<br>*We would like to have*<br>*I want the* | 3 | 6.1 | 1 | 1.6 | 1 | 2.0 |
| Bare Nominal<br>*Menu, please* | 5 | 10.2 | 11 | 17.2 | 8 | 16.0 |
| Other<br>Actual order of snacks | 0 | -- | 4 | 6.2 | 11 | 22.0 |
| Invalid | 0 | -- | 1 | -- | 0 | -- |
| Total | 49 | 99.9 | 65 | 100 | 50 | 100 |

The difference between the students from the three colleges is also reflected in their use of the polite expression "please" in addressing the waiter. As Table 17 below shows, students from MCC consistently follow the native English pragmatic convention of extending minimal courtesies such as the use of 'please' regardless of the social or economic background of the addressee. In contrast, VC students more closely follow the conventions of politeness characteristic of Indian languages, namely, using of polite forms more frequently when the addressee is one's social superior and considerably less so when the addressee is one's social inferior.

TABLE 17

*Use of the Politeness Marker 'Please'*

| MCC | % | NMRVC | % | VC | % |
|---|---|---|---|---|---|
| 41 | 83.7 | 50 | 76.9 | 25 | 50.0 |

***Situation #3*** *You are at the movie theater with some friends. You need 5 tickets. What will you say to the person in the ticket office?*

This situation also involved a low status addressee of whom a request is made. Given the relative social ranking of the addressees in the two situations, one would expect even fewer instances of polite forms here. The response patterns are given in Table 18.

The most common choice of request form in this situation was simply a noun phrase, e.g., "5 tickets (please)". However, once again, there was a difference between the three groups in their choice of strategies. Students from VC used more imperatives than the other two groups.

TABLE 18

*Choice of Formulae in Requesting Movie Tickets*

| *Constructions* | *MCC* | *%* | *NMRVC* | *%* | *VC* | *%* |
|---|---|---|---|---|---|---|
| Imperatives<br>*Give me 5 tickets* | 8 | 16.3 | 10 | 15.4 | 13 | 26.0 |
| Possibility/Permission<br>*Can/May/Could I have . . .* | 9 | 18.4 | 4 | 6.2 | 3 | 6.0 |
| Ability/Willingness<br>*Can/Could/you give me . . .* | 5 | 10.2 | 2 | 3.1 | 5 | 10.0 |
| Desiderative<br>*I/we want/need . . .* | 5 | 10.2 | 6 | 9.2 | 1 | 2.0 |
| Bare Nominal<br>*Five tickets* | 22 | 44.9 | 42 | 64.6 | 25 | 50.0 |
| Other<br>*Are tickets available?* | 0 | -- | 1 | 1.5 | 3 | 6.0 |
| Total | 49 | 100 | 65 | 100 | 50 | 100 |

**Situation #4:** *You are on Commercial Street, buying clothes (sarees, shirts, etc.) for yourself. You want the shop-keeper to show you the latest designs. What will you say to the shop-keeper?*

Given the location of the shop (also in the "Cantonment" area, like Koshy's restaurant), this situation involved a fashionable, relatively more Westernized context. The semantic formulae used for requesting in this situation are given in Table 19 below.

**TABLE 19**

***Choice of Formulae in Shopping***

| *Constructions* | *MCC* | *%* | *NMRVC* | *%* | *VC* | *%* |
|---|---|---|---|---|---|---|
| Imperative<br>*Show me . . .* | 13 | 26.5 | 21 | 32.3 | 23 | 46.0 |
| Permission Directive<br>*Can/May/Cd. I see . . .* | 9 | 18.4 | 6 | 9.2 | 4 | 8.0 |
| Ability/Willingness<br>*Will/Can/you show . . .* | 22 | 44.9 | 31 | 47.7 | 19 | 38.0 |
| Desiderative<br>*I want/wd like to see . . .* | 5 | 10.2 | 6 | 9.2 | 2 | 4.0 |
| Other<br>Info. Q + Polite Imp. | 0 | ___ | 1 | 1.6 | 2 | 4.0 |
| Total | 49 | 100 | 65 | 100 | 50 | 100 |

The data in Table 19 calls for several comments. First, we notice the by-now familiar difference between VC students on the one hand and students from the other two colleges on the other in the use of imperatives. Vijaya College students tended to use as many direct imperatives (46%) as indirect questions involving ability/willingness requests (46%), while students from MCC and NMRVC overwhelmingly chose indirect question requests, (63.3% and 56.9% respectively). However, the difference is not as marked as in earlier situations. The increased use of imperatives by MCC and NMRVC students (26.5% and 32.3% respectively) is perhaps to be explained as follows. In Indian shops, especially the more affluent ones, the clothes are shown to the customers by a low-paid attendant rather than by the shop-keeper himself. Requesting in this situation, therefore, calls for minimum politeness. (Recall that even imperatives are acceptable polite requests in Indian languages).

The next situation also involved a Westernized setting, but the addressee is not low-status but relatively high status.

***Situation #5*** *You are in the British Council Library and cannot find a particular book. You need it urgently. What will you say to the person at the desk (you want his help)?*

The British Council library, which (unlike most local libraries) charges a membership fee and carries only English books, is also located in the Westernized part of Bangalore. Most (80%) of the respondents are not members of this library, nor are they frequent users of this facility. It is used mainly by ambitious, upper middle-class students. The specialized setting of this small, elitist library contrasts with the anonymity of a movie theater ticket counter. The library clerk, being an educated professional, and usually speaking English with a native-like accent and fluency, is of a decidedly higher status than the restaurant waiter, the shop attendant or the clerk at the ticket counter. The patterns of response are given in Table 20.

**TABLE 20**

*Choice of Formulae in the British Council Library*

| *Constructions* | *MCC* | *%* | *NMRVC* | *%* | *VC* | *%* |
|---|---|---|---|---|---|---|
| Imperatives<br>*(Please get me) . . .* | 0 | -- | 2 | 3.1 | 5 | 10.4 |
| Ability/Willingness<br>*Can/Could/you help . . .* | 37 | 80.4 | 49 | 76.6 | 26 | 54.1 |
| *Will you help me . . .* | 5 | 10.9 | 10 | 15.6 | 12 | 25.1 |
| Information Q.<br>*Do you have x . . .*<br>*Where can I find x . . .* | 3 | 6.5 | 3 | 4.7 | 5 | 10.4 |
| Desiderative | 1 | 2.2 | 0 | -- | 0 | -- |
| No Answer | 3 | -- | 1 | -- | 2 | -- |
| Total | 49 | 100 | 65 | 100 | 50 | 100 |

As expected, very few imperatives were employed in this situation, although, once again, there was a difference between Vijaya College and the other two colleges. As many as 10.4% of the respondents from VC used imperatives, while only 3% from NMRVC and none from MCC used them.

A noteworthy aspect of the requesting strategy, distributed fairly evenly among the subjects of the three colleges, though VC students used more of this structure (22%), is the use of the modal question, "Will you . . . ?". While this expression would be regarded as petulant or rude in a native English context, it does not necessarily carry that social meaning in the Indian English context. Indian English speakers are genuinely confused about the distinctions between *can, could, will, would, will, shall, may,* etc., since no satisfactory grammatical account of these is available in pedagogical materials. Therefore, when an Indian English speaker uses a "Will you . . .?" question, he or she is not necessarily being rude. Rather he/she is only using the equivalent of a question form in the native language.

The next situation involved a neutral setting with a child as the addressee, and the request was for the time of day.

***Situation #6:*** *You are on your way to college and you are a bit late. You realize you have left your watch at home. A young school boy wearing a watch passes by. You really want to know how late you are. What will you ask the school boy?*

In this situation, in Indian languages, a simple information question, with perhaps an attention getter or the vocative 'boy', will do, since the addressee is younger than the speaker. The responses (summarized in Table 21 below) show that the single most frequently used (40-50%) structure is the direct information question ("What's the time?"), without any preliminaries or embellishments.

The other half of the students use some form of an indirect question, though students from VC, once again, are less likely to use indirect questions for requests. Since the addressee is a young boy, it is not surprising that as many as 14% of the respondents from VC used a "bare nominal" (e.g., "Time (please)?") to request the time. The use of "epistemic/permissive questions" such as "May I know . . ." by a third of the MCC students is a little unexpected in that that structure would be regarded as overly polite when addressed to someone younger than oneself in the Indian context.

One also sees an attempt by students from VC to express in English the equivalents of various address forms used in Indian languages as palliatives to the imperative. Some of the expressions used were: "Dear," "Hello," "Child," "Dear friend," "Aay," "Hey," "Hi," etc. As many as 8 (16%) of the respondents used one or more of these forms in their requests. Awkwardness in the choice of address forms reflects lack of emphasis on spoken English and informal registers in the present educational system.

**TABLE 21**

***Formulae used for Requesting Time***

| *Constructions* | *MCC* | *%* | *NMRVC* | *%* | *VC* | *%* |
|---|---|---|---|---|---|---|
| *Imperatives*<br>*(Please) tell me . . .* | *1* | *2.0* | *1* | *1.5* | *0* | -- |
| Epistemic Questions<br>*May/Can I know . . .* | 19 | 38.8 | 16 | 24.6 | 11 | 22.0 |
| Willingness/Ability<br>*Can/Could/Would you . . .* | 8 | 16.4 | 17 | 26.2 | 7 | 14.0 |
| Info. Questions<br>*What's the time?*<br>*Is it past nine?* | 20 | 40.8 | 27 | 41.5 | 25 | 50.0 |
| Bare Nominals<br>*Time (please).* | 1 | 2.0 | 3 | 4.7 | 7 | 14.0 |
| Other: Do you have . . . | 0 | -- | 1 | 1.5 | 0 | -- |
| Total | 49 | 100 | 65 | 100 | 50 | 100 |

***Situation #7:*** *You need a copy of your marks sheets from the Registrar's office. What would you say to the person at the desk?*

The students' responses to this situation (see Table 22) provide a number of interesting insights into the intimate relationship between the choice of linguistic form and social structure in non-native varieties.

First, note that the frequency of use of imperatives in this situation is much less than in the first four situations, even by students of VC. This reflects the Indian attitude toward bureaucracy--the feeling that the bureaucrat is doing the consumer/client a favor even when performing a service that is regarded as the client's right in Western societies. Notice also the high frequency of the use of desideratives in this situation, by far the highest in any of the seven. The students who use them seem to find it necessary to preface their request with elaborate explanations and justifications by way of coaxing the bureaucrat to accede to their request.

**TABLE 22**

***Choice of Formulae in Requesting for Marks Sheet***

| *Constructions* | *MCC* | *%* | *NMRVC* | *%* | *VC* | *%* |
|---|---|---|---|---|---|---|
| Imperatives<br>*Give me (please) . . .* | 5 | 10.4 | 2 | 3.1 | 4 | 8.0 |
| Permission Directives<br>*Can/May I have . . .* | 16 | 33.3 | 26 | 40.0 | 10 | 20.0 |
| Ability/Willingness<br>*Can/Would/Could you . . .* | 8 | 16.7 | 19 | 29.2 | 15 | 30.0 |
| Desiderative<br>*I need/want a . . .* | 19 | 39.6 | 18 | 27.7 | 20 | 40.0 |
| Bare Nominals<br>*Marks sheet (please) . . .* | 0 | -- | 0 | -- | 1 | .0 |
| No Answer | 1 | -- | 0 | -- | 0 | -- |
| Total | 49 | 100 | 65 | 100 | 50 | 100 |

In this situation, the difference between the respondents from the various colleges is not so obvious in the choice of formulae as such, but in the degree of elaboration of the request. Students from VC in particular gave verbose explanations either prior to stating their request, or immediately following their request, while students from the other colleges did not find it necessary to do so.

The choice of specific semantic formulae as well as the degree of elaboration of speech acts is dictated by the nature of the relationship between the interlocutors. Indian English speakers seem to find it necessary to explain their need for a service in situations such as the one in question and do not take for granted their right to demand that service. In general (and this is true of performance of speech acts in the native variety as well), the more servile the position of the speaker with respect to the addressee and the less confident a claim the speaker feels he/she has to the service requested, the greater the elaboration of the statement. Thus there is a relationship between choice of sentence formula and the interlocutor's relative position in the social structure.

The above point is illustrated in the wording of some of the requests:

"I kindly request you sir, will you show me a copy of my marks sheets please? I am in need of it."
"Excuse me, kind Sir, I need to have a copy of my marks sheet. Could you tell me whom should I contact for the same?"
"Would you kindly let me know where the copies of the marks sheets are being issued?"
"Excuse me, sir, will you grant me a copy of my marks sheet which is in the Registrar's office."
"I want to know my marks. Could you just give me a copy of my marks sheet?"

It is fascinating to study the choice of lexical items in these (and indeed all of) Indian English sentences. Consider, for example, the register confusion in the use of "I kindly request you, sir", the archaism of "kind sir", the palliative "just" among other things. However, I will not pursue that analysis here.[6]

## 4. GENERAL DISCUSSION

Having analyzed the choice of request strategies in each situation, let us now examine the patterns of response in relation to one another. Table 23 gives a comparative statement of the choice of strategies across situations (see note 7 for explanations of abbreviations).

**TABLE 23**

*Choice of Semantic Formulae by Situations*

Constructions

| Sit | Nom | Imp | Perm | Abl/Wil | Des | Info.Q | Oth | Inv | Total |
|---|---|---|---|---|---|---|---|---|---|
| 1. | 3 | 24 | 112 | 13 | 9 | 0 | 2 | 1 | 164 |
| 2. | 24 | 35 | 75 | 9 | 5 | 0 | 15 | 1 | 164 |
| 3. | 89 | 31 | 16 | 12 | 12 | 0 | 4 | 0 | 164 |
| 4. | 0 | 57 | 19 | 72 | 13 | 0 | 3 | 0 | 164 |
| 5. | 0 | 7 | 0 | 139 | 1 | 11 | 0 | 6 | 164 |
| 6. | 11 | 2 | 46 | 32 | 0 | 72 | 1 | 0 | 164 |
| 7. | 1 | 11 | 52 | 42 | 57 | 0 | 0 | 1 | 164 |
| Total | 128 | 167 | 320 | 319 | 97 | 83 | 25 | 9 | |

It is clear from Table 23 that students do show clear preferences in choice of one strategy over another in specific situations. For example, few imperatives are used in the library, the Registrar's office, and with the school boy, while they are quite common in the clothing store, the restaurant, and the movie theater. This is clearly a function of the speaker's evaluation of his/her status relative to that of the addressee. However, the use of direct versus indirect requests is also a function of the students' degree of Westernization. This is seen when we compare the use of the different request strategies by students from the three colleges. The relevant patterns are presented in Table 24.

**TABLE 24**

***Choice of Semantic Formulae by Students from Different Colleges***

| *Constructions* | *Colleges* | | | | | |
|---|---|---|---|---|---|---|
| | *MCC* | *%* | *NMRVC* | *%* | *VC* | *%* |
| Bare Nominals | 28 | 8.2 | 56 | 12.3 | 44 | 12.6 |
| Imperatives | 38 | 11.2 | 54 | 11.9 | 75 | 21.4 |
| Permission | 124 | 36.2 | 133 | 29.3 | 63 | 18.0 |
| Ability/Willingness | 92 | 26.5 | 139 | 30.5 | 89 | 25.4 |
| Desiderative | 34 | 9.9 | 34 | 7.5 | 29 | 8.3 |
| Information Questions | 23 | 6.8 | 30 | 6.6 | 30 | 8.5 |
| Other | 1 | 0.3 | 7 | 1.5 | 16 | 4.8 |
| Invalid | 3 | 0.9 | 2 | 0.4 | 4 | 1.0 |
| Total | | 100 | | 100 | | 100 |

Table 24 shows that the highest frequency of use of direct requesting strategies (imperatives, desideratives, bare nominals, information questions) is by students from VC, while requesting in the form of indirect questions is the preferred strategy of Mount Carmel College students. NMRV College students are in between the two groups, though closer to MCC.

What is particularly interesting about the response patterns summarized in Table 23 and 24 is the following. These patterns cannot be explained "away" in terms of transfer from the Indian languages. Although there is clear evidence of transfer, it seems to operate selectively. The mother tongue-like patterns are used more in *informal* situations, while patterns closer to native English are used in *formal* situations (e.g., library, university). This type of variability is reminiscent of the classic sociolinguistic correlation between contextual formality and the use of 'standard' variants, although this has not, to my knowledge, been discussed in relation to the pragmatics of indigenized varieties of English.

## 5. SUMMARY AND CONCLUSION

The major findings of this study may be summarized as follows: First, it seems to be clear that requesting strategies in Indian English are different from those in native varieties of English. This is seen most clearly in the less common use of indirect questions and more frequent use of direct questions and desiderative statements.

Second, many of the differences between native and non-native patterns of requesting have their source in the conventions of requesting in Indian languages. Thus, if variation theory is to be able to explain non-native varieties of language, the speaker's mother tongue and the socio-cultural conventions associated with it have to be recognized as a major variable, analogous to class, region, style, etc., recognized in the current paradigm.

Third, even when a non-native variety uses a structure that is apparently identical to one that may be employed in a native variety, the "social meaning" of that structure may be different in the two contexts. This is illustrated by the use of the "Will you. . . ." question in Indian English. Thus, pragmatic "meaning" is not inherent in the structures themselves, but is assigned variably by the socio-cultural matrix of use.

Fourth, variation studies must pay attention not only to the differences between native and non-native varieties, but also to variation within non-native varieties. In this connection, socio-cultural factors such as *degree of Westernization* and *stratification with the non-native society* function as variables differentiating one variety of non-native English from another. Again, this is a neglected aspect in the study of indigenized varieties of English, where only regional and proficiency-based sub-varieties have been discussed so far.

Fifth, one of the most important differences between native and non-native varieties is that the latter involve "partial linguistic/communicative competence" (See Grosjean 1982, Sridhar and Sridhar 1986). The non-native speaker does not need English to perform a great many speech functions--his/her mother tongue is used for these purposes. Consequently, a number of speech functions are performed at best "awkwardly" (from the point of view of the native speaker) but, in reality, in ways that involve a direct extension of either the limited L2 competence, or the speaker's mother tongue competence. (In this connection, it may be noted that students from VC consistently gave a higher relative rating to the mother tongue as the language they would use in most of the given situations, compared to students from the other two colleges, although the majority said they would use English in all but the first situation.)

To conclude in a becomingly modest fashion, I would like to emphasize that this has been a pilot study, and the results presented are only a "first look" and need to be analyzed carefully. I do hope, however, that this study has succeeded in identifying, in a gross way at least, the variables involved, and in demonstrating the research potential of the topic. A language like English, with its global spread and bewildering diversity of speakers and socio-cultural contexts of use, poses special challenges to theories of language variation and change: non-native varieties have to be integrated into variation theory and the structural and pragmatic features of the speakers' mother tongue have to be treated as variables. After all, in the long run, pragmatic variation may well come to be seen as fraught with greater social consequences in interpersonal interaction than structural differences.

# Chapter 9

# Language Maintenance and Language Shift among Asian Indians:

## Kannadigas in the New York Area

### 1. INTRODUCTION

This is a synchronic empirical study of language maintenance and shift from a sociolinguistic perspective.[8] Its synchronicity is necessitated by the fact that the language community under focus--the Kannada-speaking Asian Indians in New York--is one of the post-1965 arrivals in the U.S., sometimes referred to as the "new ethnics" (Saran and Eames 1980), and hence cross-generational studies can not yet be made. This study presents a detailed profile of the language situation in the first generation of immigrants that should be useful in future studies of this community. The sociolinguistic perspective permits a more delicate description of the children's competence in the ethnic language than is usually found in the literature on language maintenance. It also gives insights into the dynamics of bilingual behavior in a variety of speech situations, especially into the nature of the linguistic output available to the younger generation. This study also illustrates the value of the comparativist perspective suggested by Fishman (1966) by relating the sociolinguistic outcomes of different contact situations: Kannadigas in their home state, in Delhi, and in India and New York and other migrant groups in India.

The Asian Indian community in the U.S. offers a good opportunity for the study of the patterns of language use of an immigrant community in the first generation of its settlement. Its particular composition allows us to study several potentially important variables in language maintenance. Among these are: (a) proficiency in and respect for the mainstream language prior to immigration; (b) access to the middle and upper middle-class social roles soon after arrival; and (c) diversity of languages and regional sub-cultures within the ethnic group, including differences in the intensity of language loyalty. Additionally, it enables us to verify an important claim regarding Indian bilingualism, namely that it is conducive to maintenance rather than shift.

## 2. ASIAN INDIANS IN THE UNITED STATES

According to the 1980 Census, there are approximately 361,500 Asian Indians in the U.S. Their geographic distribution is as follows: Northeast 120,800; North Central 85,200; South 83,600, and West 72,000. As many as 95,000 live in the tri-state area of New York, New Jersey and Connecticut, out of which 27,000 are settled in New York City (mostly in Queens) and Long Island.

The Indians come from all parts of India and include Hindus, Sikhs, Muslims, Christians, Jains, and members of other religions. The largest section of this community are professionals (doctors, engineers, scientists, academics), and a sizeable body are businessmen and entrepreneurs. Their high level of education, proficiency in English, and the relative openness of the host society give them a certain amount of independence and choice in occupation and residence, thus minimizing ghettoization, except in the case of relatively less educated and skilled persons who arrive as relatives of those already established in this country. The Indians organize themselves primarily on the basis of regional (linguistic) and religious affiliations, although there are also several federations of regional organizations.

Thus, in terms of patterns of adaptation, Asian Indians are neither totally 'assimilating' (cf. Irish Americans) nor are they 'accommodating', i.e., preserving their ethnic way of life except for minimal adjustments necessary for survival (cf. the Sikhs in the U.K.). Rather, they are 'adapting', i.e., "selectively imitating the traits of the host society while retaining a distinct Asian Indian sub-culture", somewhat like the Indians in Kenya described by Neale (1974:267). This is an oversimplification, of course, but representative, I believe, of general trends.

Given the diversity of the Asian Indian community and the salience of regional languages and cultures as rallying points, it is advisable to study language maintenance and language shift (LMLS hereafter) with reference to specific regional groups, arriving at generalizations inductively. I have chosen to begin the study of LMLS in Asian Indians with speakers of Kannada for two reasons: one, my studies of language use by Kannada speakers in two cities in South India (See chapters 4 and 7) might help me to better interpret Kannada-English bilingualism; second, the existence of a systematic study of LMLS among Kannadigas in Delhi permits a comparison between patterns of language maintenance within and outside India. This study is part of a larger project, which will eventually include Hindi, Gujarati, Bengali, and other language speakers as well.

The Kannada-speaking community in the New York area (estimated to consist of about three to four hundred families) seems to be fairly representative of Asian Indian regional groups (cf. Fisher 1980, Saran and Eames 1980). Kannada is also representative of the 15 major regional or national languages recognized by the Indian constitution. It is the official language of Karnataka, one of the 25 (mostly) linguistically organized states in India. It is spoken by about 30 million people and has a respected literary tradition dating back to about the 9th century. Speakers of Kannada (referred to as *Kannadigas* by themselves) stand mid-way on the language loyalty scale, between fierce loyalty (e.g., Tamils, Bengalis) and self-denigration (e.g., speakers of some tribal languages in India) (Satyanath 1982).

## 3. THEORETICAL MODEL

The theoretical model adopted in this paper is that of Fishman (1966), which involves three major topical sub-divisions: (a) habitual language use at more than one point in time or space under conditions of intergroup contact; (b) antecedent, concurrent, or consequent psychological, social, and cultural processes and their relationship to stability or change in habitual language use; and (c) behavior toward language in the contact setting, including directed maintenance or shift efforts. Since the topic of LMLS is being studied for the first time here with reference to Asian Indians in the U.S., and since the immigrant group in question has been in existence for a relatively short time (most of them arrived in the U.S. in the last 20 years), comparison across time is obviously not possible. However, comparison across space has been attempted with reference to Kannadigas in Karnataka, Kannadigas who have migrated to Delhi, and other migrant groups of Indian language speakers.

## 4. DESIGN OF THE STUDY

This study is based on reports of language use, attitudes, socio-cultural practices and maintenance efforts of a selected sample of Kannadigas, and on observations of interactions among Kannadigas in various informal and institutional settings. The main features of the present design are: (i) detailed information has been elicited on the *use* of the ethnic language (Kannada) and the mainstream language (English) in various domains, by both parents and children;

and (ii) special attention has been paid to the degree of the children's *proficiency* in the ethnic language.

*The Instrument:*

A 55 item questionnaire was administered to 21 families of Kannada speakers. The questionnaire elicited information in the following categories: (a) demographic details; (b) opportunities for the use of Kannada in the U.S. (e.g., with relatives, friends, in Kannada gatherings); (c) indicators of rootedness in the ethnic tradition; (d) parents' use of languages in different domains; (e) the children's proficiency in Kannada; (f) children's use of and attitude toward Kannada in various situations; (g) parents' efforts toward language maintenance; and (h) parents' attitude toward the future of Kannada in the U.S.

This being a pilot study, the respondents were selected mainly on the basis of their accessibility and willingness to participate in the study, rather than by random selection. A small group of friends and acquaintances formed the pre-pilot group on whom the questionnaire was first tried out. They also provided contacts with other families who in turn suggested more potential respondents. Some respondents were approached at a meeting of Kannada Koota, the well-organized and established cultural organization of Kannadigas in the New York City metropolitan area.

In most cases the author visited the families in their homes, and one of the parents--usually the mother--filled out the questionnaire after discussing each item with the family. Since the families, true to the Kannadigas' reputation as a very hospitable people, invariably insisted on the author's having dinner or lunch with them and would not hear of just a business visit, the author was afforded an additional opportunity to observe patterns of language use among the members of the family at close range. Only in a few cases were the data gathered by mail.

## 5. RESULTS AND DISCUSSION

### 5.1 Respondents' Background

The 21 families in the sample live in the New York City metropolitan area (11 in Queens, 6 in New Jersey, 1 in the Bronx, 1 in Brooklyn, 2 in other uburbs). They include two single parent families, one headed by a male, the other by a female. Thus in the data reported below the term "parents" refers to 20 males and 20 females.

Information on age, education, citizenship, etc., was collected for both husbands and wives. Most of the respondents are in the age group of 31-50 years, with a mean age of 43.5 years for men and 38.5 years for women. The average length of their stay in the U.S. at the time of the study (May 1985) was 14.9 years for men, 13.7 years for women, and the combined average was 14.8 years. Thus the Kannadiga immigrants are relative newcomers to the U.S. Both men and women are, on the whole, highly educated, with all the men (20 in all) possessing professional degrees--in medicine (4), engineering (11), and other disciplines (5). Among the women (20 in all), 12 have a bachelor's degree, 5 masters' degree and 2 have degrees in medicine. One woman has attended 2 years of college. All the men and women, except 5 housewives, are employed full-time, and some of the housewives also work part-time from their homes (e.g., as word processors, etc.). Their occupations are as follows: 30% engineers, 15% doctors, 55% other professionals (such as business executives, computer scientists, librarians, civil servants, etc.). Although this information was not elicited through the questionnaire for cultural reasons, their estimated family income is in the range of $30,000 to $150,000, with a mean of about $40,000 $50,000--well above the national median. Eighty percent of the men and women received their high school education in India through the English medium and 95% studied through English in college. Eighty nine percent of them were born in urban or metropolitan centers in India. An identical number of respondents indicated the metropolitan cities of Bangalore, Mysore, Bombay and New Delhi as their last residence in India.

These facts are significant for what they reveal about the respondents' linguistic repertoire. The respondents' urban background and education through the English medium is suggestive of a high level of proficiency in English. The fact that in most families both husband and wife are educated, work outside the home suggests the possibility of frequent code switching between English and the home language, even in informal domains (see Kachru 1978, S. N. Sridhar 1978, and chapters 6 and 7). One effect of this code switching pattern is that the pattern of 'ethnic language at home--English outside' found in traditional immigrant groups is not as strongly present in the Kannada families. Instead, the children are likely to be exposed to linguistic input that is largely a mixture of English and Kannada. The fact that most of the respondents lived for a while outside of Karnataka before emigrating to the U.S.A., suggests that LMLS may have started well before their period studied here.

## 5.2 Opportunities for Using Kannada

A group of questions dealt with the types of opportunities available for the use of Kannada. All but one of the families have relatives in the U.S., and many have relatives in the New York area itself. On an average, each family has 11 families of relatives in the U.S. On an average, each family has "about 20-30" families from their native town in the New York area. They each also have living nearby about 5 to 10 families from their neighborhood in Karnataka, and 15-20 families with shared college backgrounds. This is explained by the fact that as many as 26 out of 38 adults were born in the two big cities in Karnataka, Bangalore and Mysore. (Two did not answer this question.)

Six families (or 26.6%) indicated that they have relatives living with them. A majority of the families (55%) report that their relatives from India visit them about once in 2-3 years. Another 30% have more frequent visits by relatives. On an average, the relatives stay for 2 to 4 months. Since the presence of a grandparent is often cited as a factor conducive to language maintenance, the respondents were asked a specific question on the length of visits by their parents. Apart from one family in which a parent lives with them and another whose parents have never visited them, for the rest, the average length of such visits is slightly over 5 months.

### 5.3 Interaction and Socialization Patterns

Data on the presence of friends and relatives is complemented by information on the frequency of interaction among the families. Two families did not respond to the questions on this topic, so the total number of respondents is 19 for these questions. About half of the respondents (11 or 57.8%) visit their Kannadiga friends in the area approximately once in 2-3 weeks and the others (8 or 42.1%) once a week.

The Kannadigas' pattern of socialization is instructive for its implications for language maintenance. Almost 43% report that they invite mostly Kannadiga visitors to their homes and 66.7% invite mostly Kannadigas but also other Indians. Only 19.5% claim that they invite Kannadigas, other Indians, and Americans--all combined --all the time. No one reported inviting mostly Americans to their homes. (Some respondents chose more than one category of response, so the percentages do not add up to 100%). The majority of the respondents invite Kannadiga friends once or twice a month (58% and 21.5% respectively). As many as 21.5% entertain Kannadiga friends in their homes more often. These data indicate that the members of the Kannadiga community keep in close touch with one another and also that they are not highly "assimilated" into the host community.

### 5.4 Maintenance of Ethnic Culture

This lack of assimilation is consistent with other behaviors and attitudes. The Kannadigas are not fond of American sports or entertainment and do not participate actively in local or national politics (although politics is discussed quite frequently in social get-togethers). Their preference is for Indian music, dance, and other forms of entertainment. Their food habits are essentially Indian, although (vegetarian) American food is sometimes consumed for breakfast and lunch. All 21 families report eating only Indian food for dinner. Two thirds of the parents say that their children eat the same food as they do, while the rest say that their children eat both Indian and American food. Slightly more than half (52.4%) of the families "never" cook meals consisting of only American food, while 28.6% claim that they do so occasionally, and 19% rarely. The majority of the families (17 or 89.5%) visit the Hindu Temple in Queens (an active center for cultural activities for many of the Asian Indian regional groups) about once in two weeks. Almost all the families attend functions of Kannada Koota, the Kannada cultural organization, with 13 (62%) claiming to attend all the functions, 5 (24%) most of them, and 3 (14%) half of them. Such functions, usually celebrations of native festivals, performances by visiting artists, and picnics, are held approximately once in two months in the area, and are well-attended.

Like the first generation of many other immigrant groups before them, the Kannadigas are ambivalent about settling down in their land of emigration. Asked whether they plan to return to India to settle down permanently, 55% answered in the affirmative and 45% were "not sure". No one said "no". The citizenship patterns reflect this ambivalence. Forty five percent of the men and 25% of the women have become U.S. citizens. The overall figure is 35%. Since assumption of American citizenship is often the most convenient means of obtaining permanent resident status for immediate relatives, it is not necessarily indicative of a commitment to settle down in the U.S. It is interesting to note that in only two families are both husband and wife U.S. citizens.

### 5.5 Parents' Use of Language

An important aim of this study is to document, in as much detail as possible, the patterns of language use in the first generation of Kannada immigrants. This is useful for two reasons: it will enable us to fix a realistic point of reference against which the subsequent generations' patterns of maintenance or shift can be measured; it also helps to determine whether language shift begins in the first generation itself, which, in turn, influences the quality of input available to the children in their maintenance efforts.

Several items on the questionnaire focused on the parents' use of Kannada, English, or both in various informal domains. Parents reported that when Kannadiga friends visit them, the conversation is "mostly in Kannada but with a lot of English mixed in" 57.1% of the time. The other half of the respondents were equally divided between "mostly in Kannada" (23.8%) and "completely in Kannada" (19%). A similar pattern of language use is found in phone conversations as well. The same majority reported that when Kannadiga friends call them on the telephone, they use both English and Kannada, while 42.86% report that they speak mostly in Kannada.

In writing letters to relatives and friends back home, an interesting pattern of language use emerges. Kannada is the almost exclusive choice of language when the addressee is the respondent's mother (93.75%), but English is used quite often in writing to fathers and siblings. English is also the preferred language with friends. But even here, code switching is prevalent, as illustrated below. (The N in the following Table represents the number of respondents who answered these questions). The N does not always add up to 20 because in some cases the respondents either did not complete this question or their parents were deceased, etc).

**TABLE 25**

***Parents' Language of Correspondence***

| *Addressee* | *Kannada* | *English* | *Sometimes Kan.* Sometimes Eng. | *N* |
|---|---|---|---|---|
| father | 56% | 25% | 19% | 16 |
| mother | 94% | 0% | 6% | 16 |
| brothers | 42% | 37% | 21% | 19 |
| sisters | 50% | 25% | 25% | 16 |
| friends | 21% | 43% | 36% | 14 |

The use of Kannada in reading and entertainment is not very impressive. On an average each respondent had read only 2-3 books in the last two years, and most of them did not answer a similar question on Kannada feature magazines or newspapers, probably because they are not available in this country. However, an impressive 85% of the respondents subscribe to the new feature magazine, *Amerikannada*, devoted to promotion of Kannada language and culture in the U.S. As for movies, most respondents report watching Hindi movies, since few Kannada movies are ever screened in this country. About half the respondents report that they watch Kannada movies on VCR's occasionally. Kannada, therefore, seems to be mainly the language of face to face interaction among friends and relatives in this country. Kannada is also used at the functions organized by Kannada Koota as well as at other informal cultural events such as concerts, dance performances, picnics, etc. Most of the proceedings at formal cultural gatherings are conducted in Kannada (cf. Fisher 1980). However, it is not uncommon to switch over to English while discussing parliamentary procedures and other such official or legal matters. A part of the proceedings is often conducted in English in order to include and encourage participation by children. This was a controversial decision when it was first taken, and some members consider this procedure conducive to language shift if not an implicit admission of the inevitability of the shift.

Religion is usually one of the strongest bastions of the ethnic tongue. However, it plays a rather marginal role in the maintenance of Kannada because of the strong dichotomy between ritual and prayer in the Hindu tradition. While the language of formal ritual is Sanskrit, the mother tongue is used for personal prayers, group songs, devotional hymns and expositions of religious or mythological subjects. In the Hindu Temple in New York, the language of ritual is Sanskrit, but all the other religious activities are left to the initiative of the individual or interested groups of people. All of the respondents in the sample are Hindus; most seem to be religious (for example, most homes have a portion of a room designated as "the gods' room" or a shrine), yet few specifically religious gatherings take place in which Kannada is used. The singing of Kannada devotional songs is very popular, but this is done as part of frequently held concerts of vocal Karnatic music and has little religious significance. Few traditional bards (narrator-singers of *Harikathe*'s) visit this country. Hence religion is marginal to the maintenance of Kannada.

To summarize this section, Kannada is used very much in the family domain, in face to face and telephone interactions among relatives and friends, and at Kannada functions, but it frequently shares this privilege with English. There is extensive code mixing of English with Kannada in all domains. Kannada has no place in domains such as the workplace and in formal education. Against this background of parental use of Kannada, let us now consider the patterns of the childrens' use of languages.

## 5.6 The Children's Use of Languages

The families in the sample have, on average, two children each. The first-born is 14.8 years old, and the second child is 12.03 years old. Seventeen percent of the total of 38 children in the sample were born outside the U.S., and 7 of them came to the U.S. before they were 2 years old. In other words, 28 out of 38, or 73.7%, learnt their first language in the U.S.

We have already seen that the parents use a mixture of Kannada and English in interacting with their friends. We will now look at the children's use of Kannada and English in detail. It is important to keep in mind that the data are based on the parents' report of language used by their children and not on the childrens' own report or actual samples of children's language use. The validity of the parents' report, however, was confirmed in several observations by the present author, though a more direct study is certainly needed. A distinctive feature of this study is the attempt to present a detailed description of the nature and extent of the children's proficiency in the ethnic language. For this purpose, language proficiency was divided into a number of functional categories including various skills such as speaking, understanding, reading, and writing in specific functional domains. Language dominance was investigated by means of questions on the extent of language mixing and the active or passive nature of the children's competence.

First of all, the parents were asked whether their children understood spoken Kannada used in everyday conversations about food, clothing, friends, etc. It was reported that all the children have this ability. Next, with regard to speaking ability, this skill was subdivided into four types of behavior ranging from minimal lexical competence to native-like fluency, with two intermediate categories involving non-concatenated speech and limited conversational ability. Data was gathered for each child for each of these sub-category of skills, as the following Table shows.

**TABLE 26**

*How well can the Children Speak Kannada?*

| *Category of Skill* | *child 1 (n=21)* | *child 2 (n=12)* | *child 3 (n=3)* | *child 4 (n=1)* |
|---|---|---|---|---|
| a. basically they speak English but mix a few Kannada words and phrases sometimes | 6 | 3 | 1 | -- |
| b. can answer simple questions in single words or phrases or a sentence, but cannot use several sentences at a stretch | 5 | 5 | 0 | -- |
| c. can carry on a short conversation about their interests, hobbies, etc. | 5 | 4 | 1 | 1 |
| d. can speak as well as native speakers from Karnataka | 5 | -- | 1 | -- |

It is often observed that the older children in first generation immigrant families are more proficient in the ethnic language than their younger siblings. This claim seems to be supported in the present data by the fact that mostly firstborns are claimed to have nativelike competence in the spoken language. There may be several explanations for this. Parents have greater control over the linguistic input directed at the first born. Also, presence of older siblings whose language is increasingly affected by the mainstream language may make the younger child's control over the ethnic tongue less secure.

Other questions dealt with the children's ability to read a short story and write a letter in Kannada. The majority of the children do not have either skill, although they are slightly better in reading than in writing.

TABLE 27

***Childrens' Ability to Read and Write Kannada***

| "Can your children read a short story in Kannada"? | | |
|---|---|---|
| Yes 23.8% | No 66.7% | Some 9.5% |
| **"Can your children write a short letter in Kannada"?** | | |
| Yes 14.28% | No 80.96% | Some 4.76% |

## 5.7 Children's Use of Kannada With Different Interlocutors

A commonly observed phenomenon in intergenerational communication in immigrant settings is that the children often have a receptive knowledge of their parents' language but rely on the mainstream language for active communication. This seems to be true of the Kannada children too. Parents were asked in which language their children answered when they spoke to them in Kannada. The responses are as follows:

**TABLE 28**

***Childrens' Response Language***

"When you speak to your children in Kannada, they answer in ____"

| *Category of Response* | *child 1 (n=21)* | *child 2 (n=13)* | *child 3 (n=3)* | *child 4 (n=1)* |
|---|---|---|---|---|
| English | 5 | 4 | -- | -- |
| English but include a few words in Kan. | 6 | 7 | 3 | 1 |
| Kannada | 10 | 2 | -- | -- |

Note that as many as 26 out of 38 (or 68.6%) children are described as not responding in Kannada. Once again, we note that the older children have a better command of the ethnic language, although the overall pattern is one of preference for English in the spoken domain.

When the families visit Karnataka, which they do once every three years on average, the children speak with their relatives and friends using both English and Kannada. (Fifty two percent of the parents report this.) A third of the parents claim that their children speak mostly in Kannada. Another 29% say that Indian (Kannada) children speak to their children in English. However, it is interesting that only 9.52% report that their children speak "mostly in English" in this context. (Some parents checked more than one answer.) Apparently, the immigrant children have not shifted completely to English.

The children consistently used more Kannada with their grandparents (who may be sometimes monolingual in Kannada) than with their parents. Nearly eighty six percent of the respondents reported that this was the case, while the rest said there was no difference.

A strong test of maintenance may be said to be the extent of use of the ethnic language by younger generations among themselves. As a background for this question, the parents were asked whether their children got together with other Kannadiga children on their own. Eighty-six percent replied, "not any more than with other children" and 14% said that their children "preferred the company of Kannadiga children". Not surprisingly, the children's pattern of socialization is more assimilatory than that of their parents. When the Kannada children get together, they almost always (90.48%) use English and seldom (4.76%) Kannada. About half the respondents (47.62%) report that their children sometimes speak Kannada among themselves "sometimes, just a few words". For the younger generation, then, Kannada seems to be mainly an instrument for *receiving* information from the older generation and English is the primary vehicle of active communication among themselves. However, they do have a positive or at least an accepting attitude about being spoken to in Kannada. Asked how the children feel about their talking to them in Kannada, the parents' response was (a) "they don't mind" (94.7%), (b) "they like it" (26.3%), and (c) "they ask us to speak English" (5.2%) in that order. (Some respondents checked both responses (a) and (b), hence the figures add up to more than 100%.)

To summarize this section, the children have a primarily receptive knowledge of Kannada, with a very restricted competence in the spoken domain. Very few can read or write. The older children are more proficient than their siblings, and the children use more Kannada with their grandparents and relatives in India, but English is clearly the dominant language for most of them both at home and outside.

### 5.8 Parents' Attitudes and Efforts to Maintain Kannada

The parents seem to be making, or have made in the past, various efforts to maintain Kannada in their homes. Two thirds of the respondents report that they "make a special effort to bring together Kannada speaking friends in [their] home so that [they] can speak Kannada". Only 2 (10%) denied any such efforts and 5 (23%) said they did so "sometimes". As already noted, most of them subscribe to *Amerikannada*, which regularly features lessons in Kannada for children. About half of them enrolled their children in informal Kannada classes offered on weekends at the Hindu temple from time to time. Describing what the children had learnt at the end of these classes, 5 parents said their children could write a few words, 1 said they could recite some poems, and 1 reported that the children could recognize a few words. Five parents did, however, claim that their children could do all these things as well as read a few sentences and write a letter. It is not clear to what extent these abilities are attributable to these classes (which are run by untrained volunteers, emphasizing rote memorization) as opposed to the parents' initiatives and efforts at home. At any rate, observations indicate that the children's command of Kannada is, on the whole, too feeble to be functional in any meaningful sense.

The parents were also asked to indicate which of a given set of different types of efforts they had made to maintain Kannada in their home. The results are given below. (Some people checked more than one answer)

TABLE 29

*Language Maintenance Efforts*

"Do you now, or did you at any time, make any effort to maintain Kannada in your home by any of the following means":

| | N |
|---|---|
| using only Kannada at home with your spouse and children | 14 |
| insisting that your children use only Kannada at home | 4 |
| telling/reading bedtime stories in Kannada | 5 |
| teaching children to read Kannada | 6 |
| teaching children to write Kannada | 5 |
| Other means (Please specify____________________). | 3 |

The primary means through which the parents attempt to maintain the language is by using only Kannada at home with their spouse and children. Fully two-thirds of the respondents report this practice. About a third of the parents also seem to try to teach their children to read and write. However, most parents reported that such efforts are unsuccessful and that after giving them an honest try for an initial period, they themselves fall into using English at an increasing pace.

Asked about their opinion on the future of Kannada in the U.S., the respondents were unanimous in their choice of the response, "it will be maintained by a small number of people". Interestingly, none of the respondents elected the option "it will disappear in the next generation". When probed further in a subsequent question about the possibility of Kannada not surviving after the present generation, few agreed with that proposition. Close to two-thirds of the people not only felt that "Kannada should be retained and nourished as a vital link to our culture", but also expressed their willingness "to take an active part in an organized effort to preserve and promote the language." More than a third (9) also wished that "our children would learn the language and use it among themselves and when they visit India". No one agreed with either the fatalistic proposition, "It is sad, but there's nothing one can do about it" or the crassly materialistic one, "Kannada serves no practical purpose in this country, so our children would be better off learning languages and skills that are more useful". These responses show a certain amount of ethnic pride and commitment to maintenance, and a certain optimism about its future that is not necessarily warranted either by the history of immigrant languages in the U.S., especially the languages of very small groups or by the actual patterns of use within their own group.

## 6. COMPARISONS

As Fishman (1966) has observed, the comparative method is central to the identification of variables affecting LMLS. Unfortunately, the current state of research on the maintenance of Indian languages within or outside India does not permit systematic comparisons. Only a handful of empirical studies have been conducted (e.g., Subramoniam 1977, Pandit 1978, Agnihotri 1979, Mukherjee 1980, and Satyanath 1982), although a number of interesting claims have been made on the basis of impressionistic observations. In what follows, an attempt will be made to examine the trends identified in the present study in the light of claims and results of available studies of Indian language maintenance.

It is often claimed that a distinctive feature of bilingualism in India is its stability, i.e., speakers of Indian languages tend to maintain their languages when they live away from the region where it is dominant. Pandit's (1971, cited in Mahapatra 1979:109) statement is representative.

> One of the typical features of multilingualism or bilingualism in India is its stability; despite the high rate of illiteracy and lack of any tradition of formal language teaching in India, the incidence of bilingualism indicates that speakers of different languages stay side by side, in considerable number in rural as well as urban areas, thereby making a sizeable population of each language a bilingual group.

A similar claim is made by Srivastava (1977:74), and Gumperz and Wilson (1971:153-4) and others. The presence of numerous small transplanted communities which preserve their languages, such as the Saurashtrian (Gujarati) silk-weavers in Tamil Nadu, the Konkani Saraswat Brahmins in Karnataka, the Marathi-speaking Brahmins in Tanjavur (Tamil Nadu), the Tamil-speaking Iyyengars and Telugu-speaking Shetty's in Karnataka, are cases in point. Indeed, the co-existence of hundreds of languages over thousands of years in the Indian sub-continent supports this view.

Many explanations have been offered for this phenomenon of maintenance. In addition to "group internal" factors such as maintenance of social ties, kin relationships ("a continuous link between the out-of-the-state community and the home-based community"), Pandit (1977:9) cites an attribute of the host community, namely the tolerant and pluralistic outlook of the Indian society as a crucial factor:

> In order to settle down among other language speakers, an Indian does not have to give up his language. He is welcome despite his different language; speaking a different language does not make him an alien. The underlying acceptability of an Indian in any cultural setting is symptomatic of cultural identity and homogeneity at a deeper level; it permits retention of identity markers- whether it is language or religion, food habits or dress habits.

Gumperz and Wilson (1971) in their study of a trilingual community in Kupwar (Maharashtra), attribute the maintenance of languages to the local norms and values that require the "ethnic separateness of home life" (p. 151) that is, a strict separation between the public and private (intra-kin group) spheres of activity. The crucial question, as Southworth and Apte (1974) rightly point out, is why "ethnic separateness" is so persistent in South Asia as compared to other parts of the world. They note that the groups who have maintained their lingusitic separateness are for the most part "rather small groups who could be said to have some particular reason for remaining separate", such as prestige (e.g., Brahmins), particular occupational identification (e.g., goldsmiths, silk-weavers) or enforced separation (e.g., in the case of traditional untouchables).

Subramoniam's (1977) study of the maintenance of Telugu by the Chetti community of rope-makers in Trivandrum, Kerala and of Tamil by Brahmins of Palaghat (Kerala) lists a variety of socio-economic factors that may be interpreted as conducive to the ethnic separateness of home life. His variables include house-bound employment, lack of schooling, intra-community marriage, residential clustering, non-migration, absence of competitiveness, preservation of business secrets (in the case of Marwaris and Reddys in Trivandrum) and maintenance of caste identity. Nadkarni's (1975) study of Konkani in Karnataka suggests that its maintenance over several centuries by the Saraswat Brahmins may be due to their attitude of "haughty aloofness" from the local Kannada-speaking majority, enabled by their prestige as Brahmins and economic independence as a "large and leisured class of land holders". He also notes that there is also very little code switching in the community.

It is instructive to examine the data on Kannadigas in New York City in the light of the preceding discussion of factors contributing to the maintenance of "the ethnic separateness of home life". As noted earlier, the Kannadigas in New York interact primarily with fellow-Kannadigas and secondarily with other Indians in contexts of socialization and recreation. Their food habits are predominantly Indian. Their cultural affiliations are mainly with Kannada groups. They keep in close touch with each other and with families and friends back home. While these features are suggestive of a relatively mild degree of assimilation, the group also exhibits several characteristics not found in the small communities which remain ethnically separate in India. One is employment outside the home, especially among women. Others are: a high level of education, access to highly valued jobs, a strong drive for upward mobility (demonstrated by the fact of emigration itself), absence of residential clustering, and the weak connection between their caste/religion and their language. The most important factor undermining ethnic separateness is the extensive use of the mainstream language in intra-group transactions even in the home domain, and the half-hearted adoption of maintenance-conducive practices of language use with children. The Kannadigas in New York, therefore, maintain separateness of home life only to a limited degree. The pattern of language use among them is part and parcel of their perceptions--and the realities--of their role in their adopted society. The Kannada parents' relaxed or liberal attitude toward the use of English by their children has to do with the socio-psychological make-up of the community. For one thing, the Kannadiga community perceives itself as an economically successful group with a clear possibility of moving upward on the socio-economic scale. Their own success in life and migration to the U.S., were made possible by their proficiency in the English language, and they see that skill as the key to success in their adopted country as well. Also, the Asian Indians in the U.S., unlike their counterparts in Britain or Trinidad, by and large, do not feel discriminated against by the host community. (This is not to say that there are no cases of discrimination. Indeed, there are, in the areas of housing, employment, religious freedom, etc. Yet, such incidents are not perceived as a threat warranting withdrawal into an ethnic cocoon). Asian Indians feel that their superior professional skills would make them welcome in the host community and that although their skin color guarantees that they will never blend inconspicuously into the mainstream, they will nevertheless be able to pursue the American dream with minimal interference. This perception of the possibility of upward mobility is clearly a contributing factor in their acceptance and encouragement of English.

The stability of Indian bilingualism may have been a product of a highly stratified social structure that continued in an essentially unchanged form for several centuries, but with the force of massive social changes sweeping over post-Independent India, we may witness patterns of language retention and adoption that may be closer to those found in Western societies. Indeed, recent studies of language use in urban areas do indicate a trend toward shift. Particularly germane to the focus of the present study is a study of LMLS among Kannadigas in Delhi by Satyanath (1982). The Kannadigas in Delhi, like their counterparts in New York, are first generation immigrants, well-educated, middle class, and employed in white-collar jobs. Based on a sociolinguistic survey of reported language use, socialization patterns, and language and cultural attitudes by 20 informants, Satyanath found that in Delhi,

> broadly speaking, Kannada is the language of intra-group communication; Hindi is the dominant language of non-institutional inter-group communication and English is generally used in the institutional domain. It is interesting to see that some Kannadigas use Hindi and English with other Kannadigas even in the home domain.

He goes on to observe that even in the home domain the use of English comes fairly close to the use of Kannada and that among the younger generation the use of Kannada decreases in all domains. He concludes that these results are indicative of a process of language shift rather than maintenance. Mukherjee (1980) reports a similar pattern of incipient shift in favor of the dominant regional language (Hindi) among Panjabis in Delhi, although that group relies less on English and more on Hindi. The Delhi Bengalis, also studied by Mukherjee, however, show a greater degree of maintenance in intra-group domains. In these same domains, they use more English than the Panjabis, but less than the Kannadigas. Their use of Hindi is the least of the three groups in question. This difference in maintenance patterns seems to be a function of attitudes toward the languages used in the community. The Bengalis seem to be more loyal to their mother tongue and more opposed to Hindi than the Kannadigas. The similarity in the outcomes of language contact situations in Delhi and in New York suggests that stereotypes such as Western societies being more conducive to language shift than India (cf. Sharma 1977, among others) need to be reevaluated to take note of extra-geographic variables such as the role of the mainstream language in the migrant's repertoire before and after migration, the migrant community's actual and perceived roles in the new society, and group differences in language loyalty.

## 7. CONCLUSION

This study differs from traditional studies of LMLS among immigrants in America in several respects. First, the focus has been the "new ethnics", i.e., the families of immigrants with superior professional skills (a requirement for immigration under the 'third preference' established by the U.S. Immigration Act of 1965). Second, the phenomenon of LMLS has been studied with reference to a sociolinguistically sophisticated concept of language behavior, namely domain analysis, rather than on the basis of global measures of 'home language' in Census statistics. Third, an attempt has been made to measure the nature of the younger generation's proficiency in the ethnic language, and their use of it in different domains. It is hoped that in spite of this study's obvious limitations, it will, nevertheless, serve as a relatively detailed account of language use among the first generation of Kannadigas in the U.S., to be used as a base-line for future comparative studies both of this and other groups.

It is necessary to keep in mind the limited scope of this study so as to avoid overgeneralizations. The New York Kannadigas are perhaps better organized and take a more active part in cultural activities than their counterparts elsewhere in the U.S. The Kannadigas themselves are only part of the mosaic that constitutes the Asian Indian community in the U.S. The Gujaratis, for example, are not only more numerous but also more diverse in their range of occupations, and like the Bengalis and Tamilians, display greater language loyalty than the Kannadigas. Only after more extensive and systematic comparative studies have been done will we be able to tell whether the "new ethnics" will maintain their languages to a greater extent or in a different manner than the traditional immigrants to the U.S.

# Chapter 10

# Bilingualism and the Creative Potential:
## Language as Medium and Symbol in the Early Novels of V. S. Naipaul

### 1. INTRODUCTION

Of the different types of expressive potential inherent in language, this paper will deal with two. These may be called the *grammatical* potential and the *social* potential. The first refers to the possibilities of creative expression residing in the phonological, morphological, lexical, syntactic, and semantic patterns of a language. ('Grammar' is used in the broad sense here.) The second potential derives from the role of language as a social instrument, an embodiment of culture, a marker of various types of identities. The two 'potentials' (for lack of a better term) are not, of course, opposed to each other. They are complementary: 'meanings' are conveyed in language through its grammar (in the wide sense) *and* through its social symbolism.

There are, of course, other 'potentials' of language: the pragmatic potential ('contextual' meaning), the metalinguistic potential ('language used to talk about language' so ably exploited by E. E. Cummings) and so on. In this paper, I will focus on the grammatical and social potentials because these are the two 'planes' of meaning that are, in my analysis, most relevant to the study of the present topic: the use and role of language in two early novels by V. S. Naipaul. A study of Naipaul's *A House for Mr. Biswas* (1961) and *The Mystic Masseur* (1957)--which deal with the problems of assimilation of the expatriate East Indian community in Trinidad--shows that his use of language contributes significantly to the literary effect in two ways. In a 'local' sense, Naipaul's experimentation with language serves to render vividly the style and tempo of an 'alien' language as well as the objects, concepts, and values of an alien culture. In a 'global' sense, language is made to serve as a symbol of individual and group identity and distance, embodying and complementing the essential conflicts in the novels.

## 2. BACKGROUND

Naipaul, a third generation West Indian of East Indian descent and the author of over a dozen novels and studies of cultures, started his writing career with works on the life of Indians in Trinidad. First, some background on the sociolinguistic situation in Trinidad, and on the plots of the novels and the languages used by the characters and the author may be in order. Bhatia (1981) shows that approximately two thirds of the area of Trinidad can be characterized as a 'Hindi speaking area'. He adds, ". . . This presents the most conservative picture of the Hindi speaking area, for Hindus and Moslems are not the only ones who employ Hindi, as a significant number of the East Indian Christian Community also uses Hindi as the first or second language" (1981:136). The indentured laborers, most of whom came from Uttar Pradesh and Bihar, brought Hindi to the islands of Trinidad and Tobago in 1845. Since most of them were illiterate, Hindi was used to promote literacy. Trinidad identifies itself primarily as a monolingual nation with English as its only official language. With no important institutional role(s) to play, Hindi has become mainly a symbol of ethnic identity among the Trinidadians of Indian origin. It is used as the main channel for the preservation and transmission of Indian culture. Currently, there are some 40 volunteer organizations that are involved in the teaching of Hindi as a second language.

Naipaul writes about the experiences of this transplanted group. Naipaul himself has this to say about his writing. ". . . It is an odd, suspicious situation: an Indian writer writing in English for an English audience about non-English characters who talk their own sort of English . . . I cannot help feeling that it might have been more profitable for me to appear in translation . . ." (1973:12). Commenting on the stylistic devices used by Naipaul, R. Hamner says, "Others have recorded but Naipaul has given us the taste and tempo of life in the Indian locations in Trinidad . . ." (1977:208). Naipaul conveys this by using a large number of "Indianisms", which are defined by Kachru, in another context, as ". . . linguistic manifestations of pragmatic needs for appropriate language use in a new linguistic and cultural context . . ." (1983a, b:2).

As a necessary background, I will present a crudely condensed outline of the two novels that are used as primary sources for this study and their multilingual setting.

*A House for Mr. Biswas* (*HB* hereafter) covers the life span of Mr. Biswas. Mr. Biswas' parents are first generation immigrants to Trinidad.[9] The trials and tribulations of this newly arrived immigrant family are the main focus until Mr. Biswas grows up and marries Shama, a girl belonging to the Tulsi family, and moves into her household. There is constant conflict between Mr. Biswas and almost all members of the Tulsi household, including his wife Shama, and eventually his children. Mr. Biswas' greatest ambition is to own a house and move as far away from the Tulsi household as possible. His problems and frustrations as he tries to realize his dream form the main plot of the novel.

The second novel, *The Mystic Masseur* (*MM* hereafter), deals with Ganesh, his wife Leela, her father Ramlogan, and a few others. Ganesh and Leela have no children, nor a comparable extended family such as the Tulsi household. Ganesh starts out as a 'mystic masseur', and in this capacity earns the faith and respect of the local residents. This respect leads them to elect him as their governor, and Ganesh's growth as a politician and his coping with upward mobility become the focus of the novel.

The language background of the setting in the two novels is complex. There are basically four languages or varieties used: Hindi; Trinidad English; the sub-variety of Trinidad English ('the dialect') used by Indians who are not completely assimilated; and standard English. Mr. Biswas grows up speaking Hindi, but gives it up in favor of Trinidad English after he begins to go to school. His mother speaks only Hindi. The language of the Tulsi household is also Hindi, though Mr. Biswas' wife Shama speaks Hindi to her relatives and the dialect with her husband until the couple moves out of the Tulsi household. Then she and the children come to adopt Trinidad English as their regularly used language. Ganesh and Leela can speak Hindi but do not. They speak the local dialect and eventually move toward the use of standard English.

## 3. LANGUAGE AS MEDIUM: THE GRAMMATICAL POTENTIAL

I will now turn to Naipaul's creative use of the grammatical potential of English to portray the 'exotic' Indian community. Naipaul uses a number of devices in his writings to suggest the Indianness of his characters. These include calquing, agentive nominals, generic reference, borrowing, novel collocations, hybrid formations, reduplication, among others. I shall briefly discuss some of these devices and their functions next.

### 3.1 Calquing

One of the more frequently used devices is calquing or literal translation into English of expressions in Hindi. For example,

"You drive your wife away when she is *heavy-footed*" (Hb: 18) (cf. Hindi *pav bhari*, pregnant).

"*Black age* has come" (Hb: 19) (cf. Hindi *kal yuga:* an age in mythology marked by corruption and sin).

"*Draw* your photo now" (Hb: 32) (cf. Hindi, *tasvir khico*, take a photograph).

"*Nose-flower*" (Hb: 18) (refers to Hindi *nakphul*, the gold nose-ring worn by traditional Indian married women).

When Mrs. Tulsi decides to send one of her sons to England, the townspeople criticize her, saying they would have nothing more to do with a woman who was proposing to send her son across the *black water* (Hb: 19). Here, the term *black water* (Hindi *kala pani*) refers to the ocean, the crossing of which was taboo among the orthodox Hindus. However, in using the Hindi phrase, Naipaul underlines the irony of the values of expatriate Indians because they seem to have forgotten that they themselves have broken the taboo by coming to Trinidad in the first place. Calquing is ideally suited to convey the irrelevance of the value represented by the fossilized old world term in the context of the new world expression.

### 3.2 Agentive Nominals

Naipaul's characters make frequent use of agentive nominals indicating professions, e.g., *cow-herd*, *leather-worker*, *grass-cutter*, etc (Hb: 105, 208). In these examples, it is not the structure or the form of the expressions that is noteworthy but their function. In Indian languages, these professional labels carry low or no prestige, and evoke negative connotations, similar to "good for nothing", etc. Said in Hindi, they are commonly used as words of abuse. These connotations, of course, do not obtain in their English counterparts. Once again the use of such expressions in a derogatory sense by Naipaul's characters serves a dual purpose. It is both an accurate rendering of the flavor of Indian colloquial speech and also an implicit statement of a value system. These examples also illustrate why the intelligibility of a language used for cross-cultural communication needs to be studied not merely in terms of grammatical well-formedness, but also in terms of shared assumptions and connotations.

### 3.3 Generic Reference

The traditional attitude of Indians toward widows as inauspicious creatures is captured by the author by referring to them by the generic term 'widows.' The Hindi word for a widow is *vidhwa*, and widows used to be, and in some quarters still are, referred to as such. The reference in the following passage is to the widowed sisters of the Tulsi household. The readers are informed, ". . . but the widows united, and after much whispered discussion and ostentatious silence when other sisters, husbands, or their children were near, the widows announced that they were going to start a chicken farm . . ." (Hb: 378). The term 'widow' is used extensively by the author, but never once are they identified as individuals. They are treated as less than humans in the traditional Hindu society, and the continuation of that attitude in Trinidad is represented by the generic reference.

## 3.4 Borrowing

The author uses a number of Hindi words directly instead of translating them into English. These include, for example, *pandit* (priest); *puja* (religious ceremony); *chulha* (earthen oven); *toupee* (cap); *dhoti* (men's lower garment); *maharajin* (term of address for the lady of the house); *rakhshas* (demons); *Panchayat* (council of elders); *baba*, *rishi* (spiritual or religious people); *kali yuga*, *sat yuga*, *ram rajya* (epochs believed to be characterized by evil, truth, integrity, respectively); *gao mata* (the sacred cow), among others. The borrowings express, in the words of Yule and Burnell (1903), ". . . ideas not provided for by our own mother tongue . . .", i.e., they fill lexical gaps for culture-specific items and concepts in the native varieties of English.

## 3.5 Novel Collocations

There are a number of expressions which are grammatically well-formed but sound strange to native speakers of English, because the constituent parts do not normally collocate with one another in native English. Kachru (1983a) notes that collocations such as *sister-sleeper* are not structurally deviant from native patterns of English. The construction noun + deverbal noun is productive structurally in English compounding (e.g., fan-dancer, baby-sitter). The point of deviation, however, is that in Indian English *sleeper* is used in a particular sense in which it is not used in English. Another good example of such deviant collocations is *unlucky sneeze* which refers to the belief that the sneeze of some people forebodes bad luck. Such, persons, like Mr. Biswas, are said to have an *unlucky sneeze.* They may also be *born the wrong way* i.e., born feet-first. Another example is *top knot* referring to the tuft of hair tied into a knot on an otherwise shaven head among the Brahmins. Expressions such as *caste marks* (markings on the forehead of men to signify their membership in a given denomination within a particular caste), *sacred-thread ceremony* (initiation into Brahminhood), *house-blessing ceremony* also fall into this category. Other examples are: *fire-holes* (holes dug in the ground where fires are lit and for cooking); *half-wall* (a sort of low partition) separating living quarters from open areas). Thus Naipaul, like many other non-native writers of English (e.g., Raja Rao) extends the collocational possibilities of English to express the socio-cultural practices and taboos of the Indian society (cf. Desai 1982, S. N. Sridhar 1982).

### 3.6 Hybrid Formations

A hybridized lexical item consists of two or more elements at least one of which is from a language other than English. *Box-wallah*, *shudra-hood*, *pan-seller* (one who sells betel leaves and nuts); *miya's stall* (shop owned by a muslim); *saman-lined drive* (a driveway lined with luggage on either side) are some examples used by Naipaul (1973:58-60).

### 3.7 Reduplication

This is a linguistic feature that occurs freely in Indian languages but not so much in English. A lexical item such as a noun, verb or adverb is repeated in succession, primarily for emphasis but also to convey other meanings, such as the distributive, inclusive, iterative, etc. Reduplication, therefore, is in a different class of stylistic innovation than the processes described earlier because its function is not to identify a new concept but to represent the tempo and flavor of Hindi speech. Consider the following examples.

"They was *big big* books" (MM: 11).
"You and me going to get on *good good*" (MM: 20).
"You haul you tail away from here *quick quick*" (MM: 51).
"It don't make me proud *at all at all* (MM: 71).
"It make me feel humble,if I tell the truth, *humble humble*" (MM: 71).
"I wants it to have good furnitures and I wants everything to remain *prutty prutty*" (MM: 150).
". . . and all that people says about Indians not being able to keep their house properly is *true true*" (Hb: 349).
"You mean that you can't see that I *thinking thinking* about it *all all* the time" (MM: 71).

Another type of reduplication that occurs in Hindi, partial reduplication, is also used by the author. This involves not a simple repetition of the word as in the above examples, but repetition with a change in the first syllable, as in *kam-dham* ('work'). Other examples of this type are: "Stop this *bickering-ickering*, and let us go look for the boy", *paddling-addling*, *apologise-ologize*, Marcus *Aurelius-Varelius*, *puss-fuss* (to indicate whispering).

The two types of reduplication have different functions in Indian languages and these are imported into the English of the characters, as well. Thus, full reduplication serves to emphasize or intensify the meaning or scope of the reduplicated element whereas partial reduplication has a generalizing ("and so on and so forth") function.

## 4. LANGUAGE AS SYMBOL: THE SOCIAL POTENTIAL

Up to this point we have been concerned with Naipaul's modifications of standard English morphological, lexical, and syntactic patterns. The primary functions of these innovations seems to be the creation of verisimilitude--conveying the flavor of the community's speech patterns--and expression of culture-specific concepts and values. The formal properties of language represent, however, only one part, though an important part, of language's communicative potential. Another aspect of this potential is what sociolinguists such as John Gumperz have called the "social meaning" of language (Gumperz 1971). 'Social meaning' derives from the association of a language or a variety with values such as intimacy, distance, modernity, crudeness, power, elegance, and so on. A celebrated example of the use of this symbolic potential of language in literature is D. H. Lawrence's use of a non-standard dialect to evoke the groundskeeper Mellors' earthiness in contrast to Lady Chatterley's standard English.

A bilingual or multilingual setting is especially conducive to the exploitation of social meanings, for obvious reasons. Naipaul capitalizes on this opportunity to suggest or embody a variety of social relationships and attitudes. In fact, the knowledge or lack of knowledge of Trinidadian English and standard English, the use of Hindi or the Indian subvariety of Trinidadian English, all become symbols of interpersonal and intergroup attitudes and evaluations. In this sense, language becomes an integral part of character and conflict.

In both novels, cultural assimilation is identified with upward mobility and is symbolized by an abandonment of the ethnic language in favor of English. It is not, however, an easy or abrupt shift. The power of language as a symbol of cultural identity as well as a social resource creates ambivalence and conflict. The older generation, for example, is monolingual. Their inability or unwillingness to learn English is a reflection of their lack of commitment to their adopted land:

> In the arcade of the Hanuman House, there was already the evening assembly of old men, squatting on the sacks on the floor and . . . pulling at clay cheelums that glowed red and smelled of Ganja . . . They could not speak

> English and were not interested in the land where they lived; it was a place where they had come for a short time and stayed longer than expected. They continually talked of going back to India but when the opportunity came, many refused, afraid of the unknown, afraid to leave the familiar temporariness. And every evening they came to the arcade of the solid, friendly house, smoked, told stories, and continued to talk of India . . . (HB: 352).

Mr. Biswas' mother Bipti never learns to speak English, indicating that one could survive without English in an ethnic neighborhood. However, this leads to misunderstandings. When Bipti and her sister Tara go to the Commissioner of Oaths to obtain a birth certificate for Mr. Biswas, the sisters converse in Hindi about the exact date of Mr. Biswas' birth. ". . . Ghany (the Commissioner) could not follow their [the two sisters'] conversation. He disliked the way Indian women had of using Hindi as a secret language in public places . . ." (HB: 104). Even those women who could speak the local dialect use Hindi as a "secret language", especially when "negroes" or other foreigners are present.

If Hindi is the language of intimacy, the use of standard English with family members indicates lack of closeness. For example, the readers are told that after his marriage to Shama, Mr. Biswas used more English, ". . . there was as yet little friendliness between them. They spoke in English . . ." (HB: 104).

Choice of English in this situation may seem like a natural reflection of an everyday occurrence in a bilingual community: "code switching" depending on social distance. From Mr. Biswas, however, this is a meaningful and calculated gesture, for he loathes the Tulsi household and refuses to establish intimacy by speaking Hindi to them. "He always spoke English with his in-laws: . . . it had become one of his principles." Mr. Biswas uses language to distance himself from other Indians as well. Not wanting to be considered a commoner, he symbolically dissociates himself from them by refusing to speak their Indianized variety of the dialect.

Nor is Mr. Biswas alone in this identification of language and value. Owad (Mr. Biswas' brother-in-law), we are told, ". . . disliked all Indians from India." In Owad's own words, ". . . they were a disgrace to Trinidad Indians, they were arrogant, sly, and lecherous; they pronounced English in a peculiar way . . ." (HB: 486).

Language also serves as an instrument of bigotry in this diverse community. Those Hindus who have converted to

Christianity look down upon those who haven't. Thus, Lal, Mr. Biswas' school teacher,

> ". . . had been converted to Presbyterianism from a low Hindu caste and held all unconverted Hindus in contempt. As part of his contempt he spoke to them in broken English . . ." (HB: 486).

The following dialogue illustrates this point. Mr. Biswas' mother Bipti is asked by Lal:

> "Tomorrow I want you to bring your "buth certificate", you hear . . ."
> "Buth certificate" Bipti echoed the English word. "I don't have any".
> "Don't have any, eh?" Lal said, "You people don't even know how to be born, it look like . . ." (HB: 486).

Naipaul's accurate perception of the importance of language as a symbol of assimilation and hence, upward mobility, is understood in Ganesh's exhortation to his wife Leela,

> ". . . Leela, it is high time we realize that we living in a British country and I think we shouldn't be shame to talk the people language good. . . ." (MM: 71).

Ganesh's linguistic insecurity is all of a piece with his personal ambitions. Leela follows him with her own progression from her highly marked accent, grammar, and bizarre punctuation to mastery of an unmarked form of the local dialect and standard English. By utilizing the symbolic, social potential of language, Naipaul traces the drama of cultural assimilation in the shifting patterns of language acquisition and use. Language becomes both the medium and symbol of this cultural transition.

# Notes

[1]For a discussion of the number of users and learners of English as a second language around the world, and in IVE settings, see Fishman, et al. (1977), Gage and Ohannessian (1974), Strevens (1982) and Kachru (1986).

[2]I use the term Indigenized Variety of English (IVE) in contradistinction with the term non-native variety of English. The former term includes what Kachru has called the institutionalized varieties of English, while the latter includes second as well as foreign language varieties. For more references on IVEs see chapter 4, and Aggarwal (1982).

[3]I wish to express my gratitude to Mr. U. V. Vishwanath and Mr. S. N. K. Rao for their help in gathering the data. My sincere thanks to Professors Frank Anshen, Stewart Jones, Braj B. Kachru, Henry Kahane, Richard Smock, and S. N. Sridhar for their comments and suggestions.

[4]I am grateful to the following, without whom this study would not have been possible: The teachers from the three colleges in Bangalore who collected the data: Ms. Yamuna Rao (NMRV College), Ms. Susheela Punitha (Mount Carmel College), and Mr. V. S. Sridhara (Vijaya College); Ms. Lakshmi Murthy who provided crucial logistic support; Ms. Elaine Cromwell and Ms. Kathy Runchey, who gave their judgements on the IVE data; the American Institute of Indian Studies for awarding me a Senior Faculty Research Fellowship (1986-87) when this research was initiated; the State University of New York at Stony Brook for the Faculty Development Award (March 1988) that enabled me to work on this project; and Professors Mark Aronoff, Yamuna Kachru, Braj Kachru, and S. N.

Sridhar for their comments on an earlier version of this chapter. None of the above is, of course, to be held responsible for the interpretations and conclusions contained in this chapter. A much abbreviated version of this chapter appears in *English Around the World: Sociolinguistic Perspectives*, edited by Jenny Cheshire. Cambridge: University Press. (In press)

[5]In indicating their preferences for English, mother tongue, or both as their language of choice in the various situations, students from VC consistently rated mother tongue higher than English as compared to students from other colleges.

[6]It has not been possible to discuss the wealth of data on the use of attention getters, stylistic features of Indian English, and other related topics here. These issues will be addressed in a forthcoming publication.

[7]The following abbreviations are used in Table 23. Sit. = situation; Nom. = (bare) nominal; Imp. = imperative; Perm. = permission; Abl./Wil. = ability/willingness; Des. = desiderative; Info. Q = information question; Oth. = others; Inv. = invalid responses.

[8]This study grew out of an NEH seminar on "Language Maintenance and Language Shift Among American Ethnolinguistic Minorities" held under the directorship of Professor Joshua Fishman at Stanford University in the summer of 1984. I am deeply indebted to Professor Fishman for his guidance and support, and to the National Endowment for the Humanities for awarding me a fellowship to participate in the seminar. I am also grateful to all the Kannadigas for their participation in the study and for their hospitality, and to Professors David Cohen, James Dow, Melvin Reichler, S. N. Sridhar and Bette Weidman for various kinds of help and encouragement. The responsibility for any errors are my own.

[9]The page references in this paper are to the 1969 editions of the novels.

# References

Agesthialingom, S. and K. Karunakaran, eds. 1980. *Sociolinguistics and dialectology.* Annamalainagar: Annamalai University.

Aggarwal, J. C. 1966. *Major recommendations of the education commission 1964-1966.* New Delhi: Arya Book Depot.

Aggarwal, N. K. 1982. *English in South Asia: A bibliographical survey of resources.* Gurgaon and Delhi: Indian Documentation Service.

Agnihotri, R. K. 1979. Processes of assimilation: a sociolinguistic study of Sikh children in Leeds. England: University of York. D. Phil. dissertation

Akere, F. 1978. Sociocultural constraints and the emergence of a standard Nigerian English. *Anthropological Linguistics* 20:9. 407-421.

Alam, Q. Z. 1983. *Issues linguistic and pedagogic: hints for teachers of English.* New Delhi: Sterling.

Andersen, R., ed. 1984. *Second languages: a cross-linguistic perspective.* Rowley, MA: Newbury House.

______________. 1983a. Introduction: the language acquisition interpretation of pidginization and creolization. In *Pidginization and creolization as language acquisition.* R. Andersen, ed. Rowley, MA: Newbury House.

_______________. ed. 1983b. *Pidginization and creolization as language acquisition.* Rowley, MA: Newbury House.

Andersson, T. and M. Boyer. 1970. *Bilingual schooling in the United States.* Detroit: Blaine-Ethridge Books.

Annamalai, E. 1986. Some syntactic differences between spoken and written Tamil. In *South Asian languages: structure, convergence and diglossia.* Bh. Krishnamurti, eds. Delhi: Motilal Banarasidas.

_______________. ed. 1980. *Bilingualism and achievement in school.* Mysore: Central Institute of Indian Languages.

_______________. ed. 1979. *Language movements in India.* Mysore: Central Institute of Indian Languages.

_______________. 1978. The Anglicized Indian languages: a case of code-mixing. *International Journal of Dravidian Linguistics* 7:2. 239-247.

_______________. To appear. Convergence of literary and colloquial Tamil. In *Pakha Sanjam.* Patiala: Panjabi University.

_______________. 1971. Lexical insertion in a mixed language. *Papers from the Seventh Regional Meeting* of the Chicago Lingusitic Society. Chicago: Chicago Linguistic Society.

Apte, M. 1980. Acquisition of English syntax by Marathi learners: an investigation. Hyderabad: Central Institute of English and Foreign Languages. M. Litt. Dissertation

Apte, M. L. 1974a. Thank you and South Asian languages: a comparative sociolinguistic study. *International Journal of the Sociology of Language* 3. 67-89.

_______________. 1974b. Pidginization of a lingua franca: a linguistic analysis of Hindi-Urdu spoken in Bombay. In *Contact and Convergence in South Asian Languages.* F.C. Southworth and M.L. Apte, eds. (Special issue of *International Journal of Dravidian Lingusitics* 3:1) 21-41.

_______________. 1970. Some sociolinguistic aspects of interlingual communication in India. *Anthropological Linguistics* 12:3. 63-82.

Austin, J. L. 1962. *How to do things with words.* London: Oxford University Press.

Ausubel, D. P., J. D. Novack and H. Hanesian. 1978. *Educational Psychology: a cognitive view.* 2nd ed. New York: Holt, Rinehart and Winston.

Bailey, R. W. and M. Gorlach, ed., 1982. *English as a World Language.* Ann Arbor, MI: University of Michigan Press.

Bamgbose, A. 1971. The English language in Nigeria. In *The English language in West Africa.* J. Spencer, ed. London: Longman.

Bansal, R. K. 1969. *The intelligibility of Indian English.* Hyderabad: Central Institute of English and Foreign Languages.

Baratz, J. and J. Baratz. 1970. Early childhood intervention: the social science base of institutional racism. *Harvard Educational Review* 40.

Basham, A. L. 1954. *The wonder that was India.* New York: Grove Press, Inc.

________________. 1975. *A cultural history of India.* London: Oxford University Press.

Bates, E. 1976. *Language and Context: The Acquisition of Pragmatics.* New York: Academic Press.

Bean, S. S. 1981. Towards a semiotics of 'purity and pollution' in India. *American Ethnologist* 8:3. 575-595.

________________. 1974. Linguistic variation and caste system in South Asia. *Indian Linguistics* 35:4. 277-293.

Bhat, D. N. S. 1982. Sociolinguistics and Tulu dialect survey. *International Journal of Dravidian Linguistics* 11:2. 236-243.

Bhatia, T. K. 1987. English in advertising: multiple mixing and media. *World Englishes* 6:1. 33-48.

________________ 1982. English and the vernaculars of India: contact and change. *Applied Linguistics* 3:2. 235-245.

________________ 1981. Trinidad Hindi: three generations of a transplanted variety. *Studies in the Linguistic Sciences* 11:2. 135-150.

Bhatt, B. D. and J. C. Aggarwal. 1969. *Educational documents in India 1831-1968.* New Delhi: Arya Book Depot.

## References


Bickerton, D. 1983. Comments on Valdman's "Creolization and second language acquisition". In *Pidginization and creolization as language acquisition.* R. Andersen, ed. Rowley, MA: Newbury House.

Bloomfield, L. 1933. *Language.* New York: Henry Holt.

Bokamba, E. 1982. The Africanization of English. In *The Other Tongue.* B. B. Kachru, ed. Urbana: University of Illinois Press.

Bolinger, D. 1980. *Language: the loaded weapon.* London: Longman.

Brass, P. 1974. *Language, religion and politics in India.* New York: Cambridge University Press.

Brown, H. D. 1980. *Principles of language learning and teaching.* Englewood Cliffs, N.J.: Prentice-Hall.

Bruner, J. 1975. The ontogenesis of speech acts. *Journal of Child Language* 2. 1-20.

Chakledar, S. 1981. *Linguistic minority as a cohesive force in Indian federal process.* Delhi: Associated Publishing House.

Chaturvedi, M. G. and S. Singh. 1981. *Languages and media of instruction in Indian schools.* New Delhi: National Council of Educational Research and Training (NCERT).

Chaturvedi, M. G. and B. V. Mohale. 1976. *Position of languages in school curriculum in India.* Delhi: National Council of Educational Research and Training (NCERT).

Chaudhary, S. C. 1981. A study of the sociolinguistic factors affecting the second year intermediate tribal students' learning of English at Ranchi university. Hyderabad: Central Institute of English and Foreign Languages. Research dissertation

Chomsky, N. 1959. Review of B.F. Skinner's *Verbal Behavior. Language* 35. 26-58.

Clyne, M. G. 1967. *Transference and trigerring.* The Hague: Marinus Nijhoff.

Cohen, A. D. and E. Olshtain. 1981. Developing a measure of sociocultural competence: the case of apology. *Language Learning* 31. 113-134.

Cooper, R. L. and S. Carpenter. 1972. Linguistic diversity in the Ethiopian market. In *Advances in the sociology of language*. J. A. Fishman, ed. The Hague: Mouton.

Corder, S. P. 1967. The significance of learners' errors. *International Review of Applied Linguistics* 5. 161-170.

Crewe, W. ed. 1977. *The English language in Singapore.* Singapore: Eastern Universities Press.

Damsteegt, T. 1978. *Epigraphical Hybrid Sanskrit.* Leiden: E.J. Brill.

Darlymple-Alford, E. C. 1968. Interlingual interference in a color-naming task. *Psychonomic Science* 10. 215-216.

Das Gupta, J. 1975. Ethnicity, language demands and national development in India. In *Ethnicity: theory and experience.* N. Glazer and D. Moynihan, eds. Cambridge, MA: Harvard University Press.

________________. 1970. *Language conflict and national development: group politics and national language policy in India.* Berkeley: University of California Press.

Daswani, C. J. and S. Parchani. 1978. *Sociolinguistic survey of Indian Sindhi.* Mysore: Central Institute of Indian Languages.

David, A. 1978. Bilingual education: an alternative strategy for English language teaching in India. Hyderabad: Central Institute of English and Foreign Languages. M.Litt. dissertation.

Davidson, T. T. L. 1969. Indian bilingualism and the evidence of the census of 1961. *Lingua* 22. 176-196.

DeCamp, D. 1971. Toward a generative analysis of post-creole continuum. In *Pidginization and creolization of languages*, D. Hymes, ed. Cambridge: University Press.

Desai, B. T. 1982. A linguistic study of the English elements in Kannada-English code switching. Hyderabad: Central Institute of English and Foreign Languages. Ph.D. dissertation.

De Silva, M. W. S. 1976. *Diglossia and literacy.* Mysore: Central Institute of Indian languages.

Devasundaram, N. 1981. *Tamil diglossia.* Tirunelveli: Nainar Pathippagam.

## References


Dimock, E. C. 1960. Linguistic diversity in South Asia. In *Linguistic diversity in South Asia.* C. A. Ferguson and J. J. Gumperz, eds. Special issue, volume, Part III, 26:3. *International Journal of American Linguistics.* 43-63.

Dittmar, N. 1976. *A Critical survey of sociolinguistics.* New York: St. Martin's Press.

Domingue, N. C. 1971. Bhojpuri and Creole in Mauritius: a study of linguistic interference and its consequences in regard to synchronic variation and language change. University of Texas at Austin. Ph.D. dissertation.

D'Souza, J. 1987. *South Asia as a sociolinguistic area.* Urbana: University of Illinois. Ph.D. dissertation

Dua, H. R. 1984. Perspectives on code switching research. *International Journal of Dravidian Linguistics* 13:1. 136-155.

Dua, H. R. and S. Sharma. 1977. Language diversity, bilingualism and communication in India. *Indian Linguistics* 38:4. 210-220.

Dulay, H., M. Burt, and S. Krashen. 1982. *Language Two.* New York: Oxford University Press.

Dulay, H. and M. Burt. 1974. You can't learn without goofing. In *Error Analysis.* J.C. Richards, ed. London: Longman.

Dwivedi, S. 1981. *Hindi on trial.* Delhi: Vikas Publishing House.

Eersel, C. 1971. Prestige in choice of language and linguistic form. In *Pidginization and creolization of languages.* D. Hymes, ed. Cambridge: University Press.

Egbe, D.I. 1979. Spoken and Written English in Nigeria. In *Varieties and functions of English in Nigeria.* E. Ubahakwe, ed. Ibadan: African Universities Press.

Ekka, F. 1984. Status of minority languages in the schools of India. *International Education Journal* 1:1. 1-19.

______________ 1979. Language loyalty and maintenance among the Kuruxs. In *Language movements in India.* E. Annamalai, ed. Mysore: Central Institute of Indian Languages.

Emeneau, M. B. 1974. The Indian linguistic area revisited. *International Journal of Dravidian Linguistics* 3:3. 92-134.

______________. 1962. Bilingualism and structural borrowing. *Proceedings of the American Philosophical Society* 106. 43-442.

______________. 1956. India as a linguistic area. *Language* 29. 339-353.

Ervin-Tripp, S. 1974. Is second language learning like the first? *TESOL Quarterly*. 8. 111-127.

Felix, S. 1978. *Linguistische untersuchungen zum naturlichen zweitsprachenerwerb.* Munich: Wilhelm Fink.

Ferguson, C. A. 1982. Foreword. In *The other tongue.* B. B. Kachru, ed. Urbana: University of Illinois Press.

______________. 1970. *Language structure and language use.* Palo Alto: Stanford University Press.

______________. 1959. Diglossia. *Word* 15:2. 325-340.

Ferguson, C. A. and J. J. Gumperz, eds. 1960. Linguistic diversity in South Asia: Studies in regional, social and functional variation. *International Journal of American Linguistics* 26: 3., part II.

Fernando, C. 1977. English and Sinhala bilingualism in Sri Lanka. *Language in Society* 6. 341-360.

Fisher, M. P. 1980. *The Indians of New York City.* Columbia, Missouri: South Asia Books.

Fishman, J. A. 1971. *Bilingualism in the Barrio.* Bloomington: Indiana University Press.

______________. 1967. Bilingualism with and without diglossia; diglossia with and without bilingualism. *Journal of Social Issues* 32. 29-38.

______________. 1966. Language maintenance and language shift as a field of inquiry. In *Language Loyalty in the United States.* J.A. Fishman, eds. The Hague: Mouton.

______________. 1965. Who speaks what English to whom and when. *Linguistics* 2. 67-68.

Fishman, J. A., R. L. Cooper, and A. W. Conrad, eds. 1977. *The spread of English: the sociology of English as an additional language.* Rowley, MA: Newbury House.

**References**

Fishman, J. A., V. C. Nahirny, J. E. Hoffman, and R. G. Hayde, eds. 1966. *Language loyalty in the United States.* The Hague: Mouton.

Fishman, J. A., ed. 1972. *Advances in the Sociology of Language.* The Hague: Mouton.

Fishman, J. A., C. A. Ferguson, and J. Das Gupta, eds. 1968. *Language problems of developing nations.* New York: John Wiley & Sons.

Gage, W. W. and Ohannessian, S. 1974. ESL enrollments throughout the world. *Linguistic Reporter.* 16: 9. 13-16.

Gambhir, S. 1981. The East Indian speech community in Guyana: a sociolinguistic study with special reference to Koine formation. Philadelphia: University of Pennsylvania. Ph.D. dissertation

Gandhi, K. L. 1984. *The problem of official language in India.* New Delhi: Arya Book Depot.

Gankovsky, Y. V. n.d. *The peoples of Pakistan: an ethnic history.* Lahore: People's Publishing House.

Gardner, R. C. and W. E. Lambert. 1972. *Attitudes and motivations in second language learning.* Rowley, MA: Newbury House.

Gass, S. and L. Selinker, eds. 1983. *Language transfer in language learning.* Rowley, MA: Newbury House.

Ghosh, R. N. 1980. Indian bilingualism. In *Bilingual education.* L. K. Boey, ed. Singapore: Singapore University Press.

Gingras, R. C. 1974. Problems in the description of Spanish-English intrasentential code switching. In *South-west area linguistics.* G. Bills, ed. San Diego, CA.: Institute for Cultural Pluralism.

Giraddi, G. A. 1973. Diglossia and cultural stratification: a case study of Kannada. University of Lancaster, Department of Linguistics. Unpublished manuscript.

Gnanasundaram, V. 1983. The role of diglossia in the emergence of standard spoken Tamil. Mimeo. Mysore: Central Institute of Indian Languages.

Gonzalez, A. 1983. Towards a description of standard Singapore English. In *Varieties of English in Southeast Asia.* R. B. Noss, ed. Singapore: Singapore University Press.

Greenfield, L. and J. A. Fishman. 1971. Situational measures of normative language views of person, place and topic among Puerto Rican bilinguals. In *Bilingualism in the barrio.* J. A. Fishman, ed. Bloomington: Indiana University Press.

Grosjean, F. 1982. *Life with two languages: an introduction to bilingualism.* Cambridge, MA: Harvard University Press.

Gumperz, J. J. 1982. Conversational code switching. In *Discourse strategies.* J. J. Gumperz, ed. Cambridge: University Press.

________________. 1971. *Language in social groups.* Stanford: Stanford University Press.

________________. 1970. Verbal strategies in multilingual communication. In R. D. Abrahams and R. C. Troike, eds. *Language and cultural diversity in American education.* Englewood Cliffs: Prentice-Hall.

________________. 1964. Hindi-Punjabi code switching in Delhi. *Proceedings of the Ninth International Congress of Linguistics.* The Hague: Mouton.

________________. 1961. Speech variation and the study of Indian civilization. *American Anthropologist* 63. 976-987.

________________. 1958. Dialect differences and social stratification in a North Indian village. *American Anthropologist* 60. 668-682.

Gumperz, J. J. and E. Hernandez-Chavez. 1978. Cognitive aspects of bilingual communication. Language Behavior Research Laboratory Working Paper No. 28. Berkeley: University of California, mimeo.

Gumperz, J. J. and E. Hernandez-Chavez. 1972. Bilingualism, bidialecalism, and classroom interaction. In *Functions of language in the classroom.* C. Cazden, V.P. John, and D. Hymes, eds. New York: Teacher's College, Columbia University.

Gumperz, J. J. and R. Wilson. 1971. Convergence and creolization: a case from Indo-Aryan/Dravidian border. In *Pidginization and Creolization of Languages.* D. Hymes, ed. London: Cambridge University Press.

Gupta, S. L. 1980. University level publishing in India. In *Educational publishing in developing countries.* Delhi: National Book Trust, India.

**References**


Halbar, R. G. 1981. Bilingualism in a Karnataka border village. *International Journal of Dravidian Linguistics* 10:1. 160-179.

Halverson, J. 1966. Prolegomena to the study of Ceylon English. *University of Ceylon Review* 24:1 and 2. 61-75.

Hamner, R. D., ed., 1977. *Critical perspectives on V.S. Naipaul.* Washington: Three Continent Press.

Haq, A. K. F. 1972. *Mukti sangram* ("War of Liberation"). Dacca: Dacca University.

Haugen, E. 1972. The analysis of linguistic borrowing. *Language* 26. 210-231.

Haugen, E. 1953. *The Norwegian language in America: a study in bilingual behavior.* Philadelphia: University of Pennsylvania Press.

Hosali, P. 1982. Butler English: form and function. Hyderabad: Central Institute of English and Foreign Languages. Ph.D. dissertation.

Hudson, R. A. 1980. *Sociolinguistics.* Cambridge: University Press.

Hyltenstam, K. 1984. The use of typological markedness conditions as predictors in second language acquisition: the case of pronominal copies in relative clauses. In *Second languages: a cross linguistic perspective.* R. Andersen, ed. Rowley, MA: Newbury House.

Hymes, D., ed., 1971. *Pidginization and Creolization of languages.* Cambridge: University Press.

Ianco-Worrall, A. D. 1972. Bilingualism and cognitive development. *Child Development* 43. 1390-1400.

*India: Literacy atlas.* 1978. Mysore: Central Institute of Indian Languages.

India, Government of. 1953. *Secondary education commission report.* New Delhi: Ministry of Education.

India, Government of. 1959. *Report of university education commission 1941-1949.* New Delhi: Ministry of Education.

India, Government of. 1966. *Report of the education commission.* New Delhi: Ministry of Education.

Jain, M. P. 1974. Error Analysis: source, cause and significance. In *Error Analysis*. J.C. Richards, ed. London: Longman.

Jakobovits, L. A. and B. Gordon. 1974. *The Context of Language Teaching*. Rowley, MA: Newbury House.

Kachru, B. B. 1986. *The Alchemy of English: The spread, functions and models of non-native Englishes*. New York: Pergamon.

______________. 1986a. American English and other Englishes. In *The Alchemy of English*. B. B. Kachru, ed. Oxford: Pergamon Press.

______________. 1983a. *The Indianization of English*. New Delhi: Oxford University Press.

______________. 1983b. The bilingual's creativity: discoursal and stylistic strategies in contact literatures in English. *Studies in the Linguistic Sciences* 13: 2. 37-56.

______________. 1982a. Models for non-native Englishes. In *The Other tongue: English across cultures*. B. B. Kachru, ed. Urbana: University of Illinois Press.

______________. 1982b. Meaning in deviation. In *The Other Tongue*. B. B. Kachru, ed. Urbana: University of Illinois Press.

______________. 1982c. Language policy in South Asia. *Annual Review of Applied Linguistics*. Volume II. Rowley, MA: Newbury House.

______________. 1979. Code mixing as a verbal strategy in India. In *International dimensions of bilingual education*. J. E. Alatis, ed. [Georgetown University Monographs on Languages and Linguistics]. Washington, D.C.: Georgetown University Press.

______________. 1978. Toward structuring code-mixing: an Indian perspective. In *Aspects of Sociolinguistics in South Asia*. B. B. Kachru and S. N. Sridhar, eds. (special issue of *International Journal of the Sociology of Language* 16. 27-44).

______________. 1977. Linguistic schizophrenia and language census. *Linguistics* 186. 17-33.

______________. 1976. Models of English for the Third World: white man's linguistic burden or language pragmatics? *TESOL Quarterly* 10:2. 221-239.

**References**


________________. 1975. Lexical innovations in South Asian English. *International Journal of the Sociology of Language* 4. 55-74.

________________. 1969. English in South Asia. In *Current Trends in Linguistics*, 5, T. A. Sebeok, ed. The Hague: Mouton.

Kachru, B. B. and S. N. Sridhar, eds., 1978. Aspects of sociolinguistics in South Asia. (Special issue of *International Journal of the Sociology of Language.* 16.) Mouton: The Hague.

Kachru, Y. 1980. Transfer in overgeneralization: contrastive linguistics revisited. *TESL Studies.* 3. 152-162.

Kahane, H. and R. Kahane. 1972. Decline and survival of Western prestige languages. *Language* 55:1. 183-198.

Kanungo, G. B. 1962. *The language controversy in Indian education.* University of Chicago: The Comparative Education Center.

Kandiah, T. 1981. Lankan English schizoglossia. *English World Wide: A Journal of Varieties of English* 2:1. 63-81.

Karunakaran, K. 1978. *Studies in Tamil sociolinguistics.* Madras: Pari Nilayam.

Kellerman, E. 1978. Giving learners a break: native language intuitions as a source of predictions about transferability. *Working Papers on Bilingualism.* 15. 59-92.

Khubchandani, L. M. 1984. Sociolinguistics in India: the decade past, the decade to come. *International Journal of the Sociology of Language* 45. 47-64.

________________. 1983. *Plural languages, plural cultures.* Hawaii: East West Center.

________________. 1978. Distribution of contact languages in India: a study of 1961 bilingual returns. In *Advances in the study of societal multilingualism.* J. A. Fishman, ed. New York: Mouton.

Klein, W. 1986. *Second language acquisition.* Cambridge: University Press.

Kleinman, A. 1988. *Rethinking Psychiatry: from cultural category to personal experience.* New York: The Free Press.

Kohlberg, G. L., and R. Mayer. 1972. Development as the aim of education. *Harvard Educational Review* 42:4.

Kolers, P. A. 1966. Interlingual facilitation of short-term memory. *Journal of Verbal Learning and Verbal Behavior.* 5. 314-319.

Kothari, D. S. 1970. *Education, science, and national development.* Bombay: Asia Publishing House.

Koul, M. K. 1982. A sociolinguistic investigation in Srinagar and Anantanag. Kurukshetra: Kurukshetra university. Ph.D. dissertation.

Koul, O. N. and R. L. Schmidt. 1983. *Kashmiri: a sociolinguistic survey.* Patiala: Indian Institute of Language Studies.

Krashen, S. 1981. *Second language acquisition and second language learning.* Oxford: Pergamon Press.

________________. 1978. Individual variation in the use of the Monitor. In *Second language acquisition research.* W. C. Ritchie, ed. New York: Academic Press.

Krishnamurti, Bh. 1979a. Problems of language standardization in India. In *Language and Society.* W. McCormack and S. A. Wurm, eds. The Hague: Mouton.

________________. 1979b. Language planning and development: the case of Telugu. *Contributions to Asian Studies* 9. 38-56.

Krishnamurti, Bh., Colin P. Masica, and Anjani K. Sinha, eds. 1986. *South Asian languages: structure, convergence and diglossia.* New Delhi: Motilal Banarasidas.

Krishnamurti, Bh. and A. Mukherjee, eds., 1985. *Modernization of Indian languages used in the newspapers.* Hyderabad: Osmania University.

Kumar, A. 1982. Hindi-English code switching in academic discourse. Hyderabad: Central Institute of English and Foreign Languages. Research dissertation

Labov, W. 1972. *Language in the inner city: studies in the Black English vernacular.* Philadelphia: University of Pennsylvania Press.

________________. 1969. Contraction, deletion and inherent variability of the English copula. *Language* 45. 715-762.

## References


Labru, C. L. 1984. *Indian newspaper English.* New York: Apt Books.

Lambert, W. E., and Tucker, G. R. 1972. *Bilingual education of children: the St. Lambert experiment.* Rowley, MA: Newbury House

Lance, D. 1970. The codes of the English-Spanish bilingual. *TESOL Quarterly* 4. 343-351.

________________. 1966. Spanish-English code-switching. In *El Lenguaje de Los Chicano.* E. Hernandez-Chavez et al., eds. Arlington, VA.: Center for Applied Linguistics.

Lenneberg, E. 1967. *The biological foundations of language.* New York: Wiley.

Levine, L. 1959. Speech variation and social structure in a group of north Indian villages. New York: Columbia University. Ph.D. dissertation.

Levinson, S. C. 1983. *Pragmatics.* Cambridge: University Press.

Lipski, J. M. 1978. Code switching and the problem of bilingual competence. In *Aspects of bilingualism.* M. Paradis, ed. Columbia. SC.: Hornbeam Press.

Llamzon, T. A. 1969. *Standard Filipino English.* Manila: Ateneo University Press.

Loveday, L. 1982. *The sociolinguistics of learning and using a non-native language.* Oxford: Pergamon Press.

Lowenberg, P. 1986. Transfer as a strategy of acculturation in Malaysian English: implications for theories of second language acquisition. *World Englishes* 5:1. 71-84.

Lukmani, Y. 1972. Motivation to learn and language proficiency. *Language Learning* 22. 261-273.

Macnamara, J. 1967. The linguistic independence of bilinguals. *Journal of Verbal Learning and Verbal Behavior* 6. 729-736.

Macnamara, J. and S. L. Kushnir. 1971. The linguistic independence of bilinguals: the input switch. *Journal of Verbal Learning and Verbal Behavior* 10. 480-487.

Macnamara, J., M. Krauthammer, and M. Bolgar. 1968. Language switching in bilinguals as a function of stimulus and response uncertainty. *Journal of Experimental Psychology* 78. 208-215.

Mahapatra, B. P. 1979. Santali language movement in the context of many dominant languages. In *Language Movements in India*. E. Annamalai, ed. Mysore: Central Institute of Indian Languages.

Masica, C. P. 1976. *Defining a linguistic area: South Asia.* Chicago: Chicago University Press.

McClure, E. and J. Wentz. 1976. Functions of code switching among Mexican-American children. *Papers from the parasession on functionalism.* Chicago: Chicago Linguistic Society.

McCully, B. T. 1940. *English education and the origins of Indian nationalism.* New York: Columbia University Press.

Mehrotra, R. R. 1982. Indian English: a sociolinguistic profile. In *New Englishes,* J. B. Pride, ed. Rowley, MA: Newbury House.

__________________. 1975a. Modes of greeting in Hindi: a sociolinguistic statement. In *Studies in Linguistics: occasional papers #1.* R. R. Mehrotra and L. M. Khubchandani, eds. Simla: Indian Institute of Advanced Study.

__________________ 1975b. Matrimonial advertisements: a study in correlation between linguistic and situational feeling. In *Studies in Linguistics: occasional papers #1.* R. R. Mehrotra and L. M. Khubchandani, eds. Simla: Indian Institute of Advanced Study.

Miranda, R. V. 1978. Caste, religion and dialect differentiation in the Konkani area. In *Aspects of sociolinguistics in South Asia.* B. B. Kachru and S. N. Sridhar, eds. [Special issue of the *International Journal of the Sociology of Language*] 16. 77-91.

Misra, B. G. 1982. Language spread in a multilingual setting: the spread of Hindi as a case study. In *Language spread: studies in diffusion and social change.* R. L. Cooper, ed. Bloomington: Indiana Univeristy Press.

Misra, B. G. and H. R. Dua. 1980. *Language use in Himachal Pradesh.* Mysore: Central Institute of Indian Languages.

Misra, B. G., ed., 1976. *Studies in bilingualism.* (A study of Hindi as written by speakers of South Indian languages). Mysore: Central Institute of Indian languages.

References


Moag, R. F. 1978. Linguistic adaptations of the Fiji Indians. In *Rama's banishment: a centenary volume on the Fiji Indians.* V. Mishra, ed. Heinemann: Australia.

Mohanlal, S. and H. R. Dua 1983. Maintenance of Hebrew among the Jews in Cochin: A case study of language use. In *To Greater Heights*, Vol.II, D. P. Pattanayak and E. Annamalai, eds. Mysore: Central Institute of Indian Languages.

Mukherjee, A. 1980. Language maintenance and language shift among Panjabis and Bengalis in Delhi: a sociolinguistic perspective. Delhi: University of Delhi. Ph.D. dissertation.

Murthy, S. 1981. A study of the attitudinal function of intonation in Kannada English. Hyderabad: Central Institute of English and Foreign Languages. Research dissertation.

Muysken, P. 1984. The Spanish that Quechua speakers learn: L2 learning as norm-governed behavior. In *Second Languages: A cross-linguistic perspective.* R. Andersen, ed. Rowley, MA: Newbury House.

Nadkarni, M. V. 1977. Educational level and language choice. *Seminar in Sociolinguistics* (no editor). Hyderabad: Telugu Academy.

________________. 1975. Bilingualism and syntactic change in Konkani. *Language* 51: 3. 672-683.

Naik, J. P. 1980. *Textbook publishing and the language policy.* Educational publishing in developing countries. Delhi: National Book Trust, India.

Naipaul, V. S. 1973. *The Overcrowded barracoon.* Hammondsworth: Penguin.

________________. 1961. *A house for Mr. Biswas.* London: Andre Deutsch. (4th edition, 1969).

________________. 1957. *The Mystic Masseur.* London: Andre Deutsch. (4th edition, 1969).

Nayak, H. M. 1967. *Kannada: literary and colloquial.* Mysore: Rao and Raghavan.

Neale, B. 1974. Language use among the Asian communities. In *Language in Kenya.* W. H. Whiteley, ed. Nairobi: Oxford University Press.

Nelson, C. 1982. Intelligibility and non-native varieties of English. In *The other tongue.* B. B. Kachru, ed. Urbana: University of Illinois Press.

Nemser, W. 1971. Approximative systems of foreign language learners. *International Review of Applied Linguistics* 9:2. 115-123.

Newmark, W. 1976. How not to interfere with language learning. *International Journal of American Linguistics* 40. 77-83.

Noss, R. B., ed., 1983. Varieties of English in South East Asia. *Anthology Series* 11. Singapore: Singapore University Press.

Nurullah, S. and J. P. Naik, eds., 1964. *A student's history of education in India, 1800-1965.* Bombay: Macmillan.

Olshtain, E. and A. Cohen. 1983. Apology - a speech act set. In *Sociolinguistics and language acquisition.* N. Wolfson and E. Judd, eds. Rowley, MA: Newbury House.

Pandharipande, R. 1983. Mixing and creativity in multilingual India. *Studies in the Linguistic Sciences* 13: 2. 99-114.

__________________. 1982. Counteracting forces in language change: convergence vs. maintenance. *Studies in the Linguistic Sciences* 12:2. 97-116.

Pandit, P. B. 1978. Language and identity: the Panjabi language in Delhi. In *Aspects of Sociolinguistics in South Asia.* B. B. Kachru and S. N. Sridhar, eds. (Special issue of *International Journal of Sociology of Language* 16.) 93-108.

__________________. 1977. *Language in a plural society.* New Delhi: Devraj Chanana Memorial Committee.

__________________. 1972. *India as a sociolinguistic area.* (Gune Memorial Lectures). Ganeshkhind: University of Poona Press.

Paradis, M. 1977. Bilingualism and aphasia. In *Studies in neurolinguistics*, vol. 3. H. Whitaker and H. A. Whitaker, eds. New York: Academic Press.

Parasher, S. V. 1980. Mother tongue-English diglossia: a case study of educated Indian bilinguals' language use. *Anthropological Linguistics* 22:4. 151-162.

**References**

Parmanik, T. K. 1981. A study of the attitude and motivation for learning English at the first degree level in the district of Cuttack. Hyderabad: Central Institute of English and Foreign Languages. Research dissertation.

Pathak, R. S. 1985. Language variation in a bilingual setting: a North Indian case study. *Indian Linguistics* 46:1-2. 9-24.

Pattanayak, D. P. 1981. *Multilingualism and mother-tongue education.* Delhi: Oxford University Press.

________________. 1975. Caste and language. *International Journal of Dravidian Linguistics* 4:1. 97-104.

________________. 1973. *Distribution of languages in India, in states and union territories.* Mysore: Central Institute of Indian Languages.

Pattanayak, D. P. and E. Annamalai, eds., 1983. *To greater heights* (2 volumes). Mysore: Central Institute of Indian Languages.

Penfield, W. and L. Roberts. 1959. *Speech and brain mechanisms.* Princeton: Princeton University Press.

Pfaff, C. W. 1979. Constraints on language mixing: intrasentential code switching and borrowing in Spanish/English. *Language* 55. 291-318.

________________. 1976. Functional and structural constraints on syntactic variation in code switching. *Papers from the para-session on Diachronic Syntax.* Chicago: Chicago Linguistic Society.

________________. 1975. Syntactic constraints on code switching: a quantitative study of Spanish-English. Paper presented at the Linguistic Society of America annual meeting.

Platt, J. 1977. A model for polyglossia and multilingualism (with special reference to Singapore and Malaysia). *Language in Society* 6:3. 361-378.

________________. 1975. The Singaporean English speech continuum. *Anthropological Linguistics* 17:7. 363-374.

Platt, J. and Weber, H. (1980) *English in Singapore and Malaysia: facts, features, functions.* Kuala Lumpur: Oxford University Press.

Platt, J., H. Weber, and M. L. Ho. 1984. *The New Englishes.* London: Routledge and Kegan Paul.

Poplack, S. 1979. Sometimes I'll start a sentence in Spanish, Y TERMINO EN ESPANOL: toward a typology of code-switching. Working paper No. 4. New York: Language Policy Task Force, Centro de Estudios Puertorrinquenos, City University of New York.

________________. 1978. Syntactic structure and social functions of code switching. Working paper # 2, CUNY, New York: Centro de Estudios Puertorriquenos.

Prabhoo, L. 1979. Survey of Konkani in Kerala. *International Journal of Dravidian Linguistics* 8:2. 345-355.

Prator, C. H. 1968. The British heresy in TESOL. In *Language problems in developing nations.* J. A. Fishman, eds. New York: John Wiley and Sons.

Preston, M. S. and W. E. Lambert. 1969. Interlingual interference in a bilingual version of the Stroop color-word task. *Journal of Verbal Learning and Verbal Behavior* 8. 295-301.

Pride, J. B., ed., 1982. *New Englishes.* Rowley, MA: Newbury House.

Quirk, R. 1985. Language variety: nature and art. In *Varieties of English in South East Asia. R. B. Noss, ed. Singapore: Singapore University Press.*

*Quirk, R. and H. G. Widdowson, eds., 1985. The English language in a global context. English in the World: Teaching and Learning the Language and Literatures.* Cambridge: University Press.

Quirk, R., S. Greenbaum, G. Leech, and J. Svartvik. 1972. *A grammar of contemporary English.* London: Longman.

Radhakrishnan, B. 1980. Study of diglossia and the Telugu situation. In *Sociolinguistics and dialectology.* S. Agesthialingom and K. Karunakaran, eds. Annamalainagar: Annamalai University.

Rajathi, J. 1982. Konkani--a case for language planning. *International Journal of Dravidian Linguistics* 11:2. 367-373.

**References**


Ramunni, K. 1976. Subjective reactions to regional and non-regional English accents in India. Hyderabad: Central Institute of English and Foreign Languages. Research dissertation.

Rayfield, J. R. 1970. *Languages of a bilingual community.* The Hague: Mouton.

Report on the Seminar on Tulu. 1979. *International Journal of Dravadian Linguistics* 8:2. 381-390.

Richards, J. C. 1982. Rhetorical and communicative styles in the new varieties of English. In *New Englishes.* J. B. Pride, ed. Rowley, MA: Newbury House.

________________. ed., 1974. *Error Analysis: perspectives on second language acquisition.* London: Longman.

________________. 1974. Social factors, interlanguage and language learning. In *Error analysis.* J. C. Richards, eds. London: Longman.

Rubdy, R. 1981. A study of some written varieties of Indian English. Hyderabad: Central Institute of English and Foreign Languages. Ph.D. dissertation.

________________. 1975. Phonological analysis of English spoken by ten Marathi speakers from Maharashtra. Hyderabad: Central Institute of English and Foreign Languages. Research dissertation

Rutherford, W. E., ed., 1984. *Language Universals and Second language acquisition.* Amsterdam: Benjamins.

Sadanand, K. 1983. The use of English in industries in Andhra Pradesh: a sociolinguistic study. Hyderabad: Central Institute of English and Foreign Languages. Ph.D. dissertation.

Samarin, W. J. 1971. Salient and substantive pidginization. In *Pidginization and creolization of languages.* D. Hymes, ed. Cambridge: University Press.

Sambasiva Rao, G. 1977. Standardization process. *International Journal of Dravidian Linguistics* 6:1. 65-68.

Sankoff, G. 1983. Comment on Valdman's Creolization and second language acquisition. In *Pidginization and creolization as language acquisition.* R. Andersen, ed. Rowley, MA: Newbury House.

Saran, P. and E. Eames 1980. *The new ethnics: the Asian Indians in the U.S.* New York: Praeger.

Satyanath, T. S. 1982. Kannadigas in Delhi: a sociolinguistic study. Delhi: University of Delhi. Ph.D. dissertation.

Schachter, M. and M. Celce-Murcìa. 1977. Some reservations concerning error analysis. *TESOL Quarterly* 11:4. 441-451.

Schuchardt, H. 1891. [1980] Indo-English. In *Pidgin and creole Languages*: selected essays by Hugo Schuchardt, G. C. Gilbert, ed. Cambridge: Cambridge University Press

Searle, J. 1964. *Speech Acts*. Cambridge: Cambridge University Press.

Segalowitz, N. and W. E. Lambert. 1969. Semantic generalization in bilinguals. *Journal of Verbal Learning and Verbal Behavior* 8. 559-566.

Seliger, H. To Appear. *Strategy and tactic in second language acquisition.*

Selinker, L. 1972. Interlanguage. *International Review of Applied Linguistics* 10:3. 209-231.

Sey, K. A. 1973. *Ghanaian English: an exploratory survey.* London and Basingstoke: Macmillan.

Shanmugam Pillai, S. V. 1975. Modernization in Tamil. *Anthropological Linguistics* 17:2. 53-67.

_________________. 1965. Merger of literary and colloquial Tamil. *Anthropological Linguistics* 7:4. 98-103.

Shantha, K. M. 1977. Code switching: Malayalam-English: form and function. Hyderabad: Central Institute of English and Foreign Languages. Research dissertation.

Shapiro, M. C. and H. F. Schiffman. 1981. *Language and Society in South Asia.* New Delhi: Motilal Banarasidas.

Sharma, B. G. 1977. Indian bilingualism. In *Indian bilingualism.* B. G. Sharma and S. Kumar, eds. Agra: Central Hindi Institute.

Sharma, B. G. and S. Kumar, eds., 1977. *Indian bilingualism.* Agra: Kendriya Hindi Sansthan.

**References**

Sharma, B. N. 1985. *Medium of instruction in India.* New Delhi: Central Secretariat Library, Department of Culture.

Sharma, R. K. 1971. Tribal education in Nagaland. Proceedings of the conference of tribal research bureaus in India. Mysore: Central Institute of Indian Languages.

Sharp, H. 1920. *Selections from educational records, Part I and II, 1781-1839.* Calcutta.

Shaw, W. D. 1981. Asian student attitudes towards English. In *English for cross-cultural communication.* L. Smith, ed. N.Y.: St. Martin's press.

Singh, R. 1985. Grammatical constraints in code-mixing: evidence from Hindi-English. *Canadian Journal of Linguistics* 30:1. 33-45.

Singh, U. N. and Maniruzzaman. 1983. *Diglossia in Bangladesh and language planning.* Calcutta: Gyan Bharti.

Sivarama Murty, N. 1979. Social stratification in Telugu: a rural case study. *Indian Linguistics* 40:2. 92-101.

Slobin, D. I. 1982. Universal and particular in the acquisition of language. In *Language acquisition: the state of the art.* E. Wanner and L.R. Gleitmann, eds. Cambridge: Cambridge University Press.

________________. 1978. Language change in childhood and history. In *Language learning and thought.* J. Macnamara, ed. New York: Academic Press.

________________. 1973. Cognitive prerequisites for the acquisition of grammar. In *Studies of child language development.* C. A. Ferguson and D. I. Slobin, eds. New York: Holt, Rinehart, and Winston.

Smith, L. E., ed., 1983. *Readings in English as an international language.* Oxford: Pergamon Press.

________________. ed. 1981. *English for cross-cultural communication.* London: Macmillan.

Smith, L. and K. Rafiqzad. 1979. English for cross-cultural communication: the question of intelligibility. *TESOL Quarterly* 13:3. 371-380.

Smith, N. V. 1973. *The acquisition of phonology.* Cambridge: University Press.

Smith, N. V. and D. Wilson. 1979. *Modern linguistics: the results of Chomsky's revolution.* Harmondsworth, U.K.: Penguin.

Southworth, F. C. 1981. Detecting prior creolization: an analysis of the historical origins of Marathi. In *Papers in Linguistics.* [Dr. R.C. Hiremath felicitation volume], M. S. Sunkapur and J. S. Kulli, eds. Mysore: Sharat Prakashana.

________________. 1979. Functional aspects of bilingualism. *International Journal of Dravidian Linguistics* 8:2. 393-397.

________________. 1977. Functional aspects of linguistic heterogeneity. In *Indian bilingualism.* B. G. Sharma and S. Kumar, eds. Agra: Central Institute of Hindi.

Southworth, F. C. and M. L. Apte. 1974. Introduction. In *Contact and convergence in South Asian languages.* F. C. Southworth and M. L. Apte, eds. *International Journal of Dravidian Linguistics* 3:1. 1-20.

Spencer, J., ed., 1971. *The English Language in West Africa.* London: Longman.

Spolsky, B. 1972. *The language education of minority children. Rowley, MA: Newbury House.*

*Sreedhar, M. V. 1979. The functions of bilingualism in Nagaland. International Journal of Dravidian Linguistics* 22. 103-114.

________________. 1976. Standardization of Naga pidgin. *Anthropological Linguistics* 18:8. 371-379.

Sridhar, K. K. In press. Language policy for education in multilingual India: issues and implementations. Proceedings of the conference on language contact + conflict, June 2-4. Brussels: Center for Research on Multilingualism.

________________. 1988. Language maintenance and language shift among Asian Indians: Kannadigas in the New York area. *International Journal of the Sociology of Language* 69. 73-87.

________________. 1985a. Sociolinguistic theories and non-native varieties of English. *Lingua* 68:1. 85-104.

________________. 1985b. Bilingualism in South Asia (India): national/regional profiles and verbal repertoires. *Annual Review of Applied Linguistics*. 6.169-186.

________________. 1982. English in South Indian urban context. In *The Other Tongue*. B. B. Kachru, ed. Urbana: University of Illinois Press.

________________. 1979. English in the sociocultural context of India. *Studies in Language Learning*. 2:2. 63-79.

________________. 1977. The development of English as an elite language in the multilingual context of India: its educational implications. Urbana: University of Illinois. Ph.D. dissertation.

Sridhar, S. N. (in press) *Kannada* (Croom Helm Descriptive Grammar Series). London: Routledge.

________________. 1988. *Cognition and Sentence Production: A Cross-Linguistic Study*. New York: Springer Verlag.

________________. 1987a. Language variation, attitudes, and rivalry: the spread of Hindi in India. In *Language Spread and Language Policy*. P. H. Lowenberg, ed. Washington, D.C.: Georgetown University Press.

________________. 1987b. Language modernization. Paper presented at the second world Basque Congress, San Sebastian.

________________. 1982. Non-native English literatures: context and relevance. In *The Other Tongue*. B. B. Kachru, ed. Urbana: University of Illinois Press.

________________. 1981. Language teaching and literacy in South Asia. *Annual Review of Applied Linguistics* 2. 219-238.

________________. 1980. *Diglossia in Kannada*. Department of linguistics, State University of New York at Stony Brook (mimeo).

________________. 1980. Contrastive analysis, error analysis and interlanguage: Three phases of one goal. In *Readings in English as a second language*. K. Croft, ed. Boston: Winthrop.

________________. 1980. Cognitive determinants of linguistic structures: a cross-linguistic experimental study of sentence production. Urbana: University of Illinois. Ph.D. dissertation.

________________. 1978. On the functions of code-mixing in Kannada. *International Journal of the Sociology of Language 16*. 109-117.

Sridhar, K. K and S. N. Sridhar. 1986. Bridging the paradigm gap: second language acquisition theory and indigenized varieties of English. *World Englishes* 5: 1. 3-14.

Sridhar, S. N. and K. K. Sridhar. 1980. The syntax and psycholinguistics of bilingual code-mixing. *Canadian Journal of Psychology* 34: 4. 409-416.

Srivastava, A. K. 1978. *The language load.* Mysore: Central Institute of Indian languages.

Srivastava, G. N. 1970. *The language controversy and the minorities.* Delhi: Atma Ram.

Srivastava, R. N. 1980. Societal bilingualism and language teaching in India. *Indian Journal of Applied Linguistics* 6:2. 13-37.

________________. 1979. Literacy as a communication skill. *Indian Journal of Adult Communication* 40. 1-14.

________________. 1977. Indian bilingualism: myth and reality. In *Indian Bilingualism.* B. G. Sharma and S. Kumar, eds. Agra: Central Institute of Hindi.

Srivastava, R. N. and S. C. Bhatia. 1978. *Literacy, literacy materials their preparation.* New Delhi: Directorate of adult education, Government of India.

Stanlaw, J. 1982. English in Japanese communicative strategies. In *The other tongue.* B. B. Kachru, ed. Urbana: University of Illinois Press.

Stockwell, P. and J. D. Bowen. 1965. *The sounds of English and Spanish.* Chicago: The University of Chicago Press.

Strevens, P. 1982. World English and the world's English - or, whose language is it anyway? *Journal of the Royal Society of Arts.* June. 412-428.

________________. 1980. *Teaching English as an international language.* London: Oxford University Press.

Subramoniam, V. I. 1977. A note on the preservation of the mother tongue in Kerala. In *Indian Bilingualism.* B. G. Sharma and S. Kumar, eds. Agra: Central Hindi Institute.

## References

Tay, M. W. J. and A. F. Gupta. 1983. Towards a description of standard Singaporean English. In *Varieties of English in Southeast Asia.* R. B. Noss, ed. Singapore: Singapore University Press.

Taylor, B. 1975. The use of overgeneralization and transfer learning strategies by elementary and intermediate students in ESL. *Language Learning* 25. 73-109.

Thumboo, E. 1985. English literature in a global context. In *English in the World.* R. B. Noss, ed. Cambridge: Cambridge University Press.

Timm, L. A. 1975. Spanish-English code-switching: El porque y how-not-to. *Romance Philology* 28. 473-482.

Tongue, R. K. 1974. *The English of Singapore and Malaysia.* Singapore: Eastern Universities Press.

Trudgill, P. 1975. *Accent, Dialect, and the School.* London: Arnold.

________________. 1974. *Sociolinguistics: an Introduction.* Harmondsworth, England: Penguin.

Trueba, H. T. 1977. Bilingual-bicultural education: an overview. In *Handbook on Curriculum.* L. Robin, ed. Boston: Allyn and Bacon.

Ubahakwe, E. 1979. Adapting the role of the English language in Nigerian education. In *Varieties and functions of English in Nigeria.* E. Ubahakwe, ed. Ibadan: African Universities Press.

Ullrich, H. 1982. Rural and urban multilingualism: a South Indian case. *International Journal of the Sociology of Language* 34. 25-50.

*Universities Handbook, India.* 1981-82. New Delhi: Association of Indian Universities.

Ure, J. M. and S. Velayudhan, eds., 1985. *Perspectives on English language teaching.* New Delhi: Macmillan.

Vaid, J. 1980. The form and function of code-mixing in Indian films. *Indian Linguistics* 41:1. 37-44.

Verma, S. K. 1976. Code-switching: Hindi-English. *Lingua* 38. 153-165.

Walwadkar, R. 1984. Error Analysis: the use of overgeneralization and transfer as learning strategies in the acquisition of negation, yes/no questions and wh-questions. Hyderabad: Central Institute of English and Foreign Languages. M. Litt. Dissertation

Weinrich, U. 1957. Functional aspects of Indian bilingualism. *Word* 13:2. 203-233.

_______________. 1963. *Languages in contact: findings and problems.* New York: Linguistic Circle of New York.

Wentz, J. 1977. Some considerations in the development of a syntactic description of code switching. Urbana: University of Illinois. Ph.D. dissertation

Weir, A. L. 1982. Style range in new English literatures. In *The Other Tongue: English Across Cultures.* B. B. Kachru, ed. Urbana: University of Illinois Press.

Whiteley, W. H. 1974. *Language in Kenya.* Nairobi: Oxford University Press.

Whitworth, G. C. 1907. *Indian English: An Examination of the Errors of Idioms made by Indians in Writing English.* Letchworth, Herts: Garden City Press.

Wolfson, N. and E. Judd, eds., 1983. *Sociolinguistics and language acquisition.* Rowley, MA: Newbury House.

Wong, I. F. 1983. Simplification features in the structure of colloquial English. In *Varieties of English in Southeast Asia.* R. B. Noss, ed. Singapore: Singapore University Press.

_______________. 1982. Native speaker English for the Third World today? In: J. B. Pride (ed.), *New Englishes.* Rowley, MA: Newbury House.

Young, R. and I. Navar. 1968. Retroactive inhibition with bilinguals. *Journal of Experimental Psychology* 77. 109-115.

Yule, H. and A. C. Burnell. 1903. *Glossary of colloquial Anglo-Indian words and phrases, and of kindred terms, etymological, historical, geographical, and discursive.* London: John Murray. (2nd ed., edited by William Crooke).

# Index